MORE ADVANCE PRAISE ~~FOR~~ ~~U~~

"The women on these pages have as much to tell us now as they did then. Tamam has created a new genre of Islamic literature. Through her poetry she draws us to the Mothers of Islam by illustrating, exemplifying, and embodying actual human beings. Her vibrant words provide a doorway to the Wives of the Prophet."

— Arthur Buehler, Ph.D. Harvard University and Senior Lecturer, Islamic Studies, Victoria University, Wellington, New Zealand

"Untold transports the reader into the lives of the women married to Prophet Muhammad. Here is a compelling, yet subtle marriage of history and poetry that highlights the vital contribution Muslim women have made to Islamic civilization. I recommend this good and unusual book."

— Daisy Khan, Executive Director of the American Society for Muslim Advancement (ASMA), and Founder of Woman's Islamic Initiative in Spirituality and Equality (WISE).

"'Paradise lies beneath the feet of the Mothers,' said Muhammad. In this powerful, poetic history Tamam Kahn brings to life the world where those feet walked, the ground the Mothers of Islam had to hold with fierceness, tenderness, and passion. … In Tamam Kahn the Mothers of Islam have found a beautiful, authentic voice."

— Elizabeth Cunningham, author of *The Passion of Mary Magdalen*

"To read through *Untold* is like making a journey through a broad, colorful, desert landscape, as one is carried along in prose and then halted by sudden encounters with personages who eagerly tell their stories, or by striking features of landscape that offer themes and images for contemplation. When the journey provides understanding, the abrupt bursts of poetry offer exhilaration. Each is indispensable to the other."

— Fred Chappell, former Poet Laureate of North Carolina and author of *Shadow Box*

UNTOLD

UNTOLD

A History of the Wives
of
Prophet Muhammad

Tamam Kahn

Best wishes Tamam Kahn

Monkfish Book Publishing Company
Rhinebeck, New York

Cover art by Halla Ayla
http://hallaayla.com/

Book and cover design by Georgia Dent
Author photograph by Aya Brackett

The author wishes to thank the following for kind permissions granted:

Naomi Shihab Nye; "Kindness," *Words Under the Words: Selected Poems*, Portland, The Eighth Mountain Press, 1995.

Eavan Boland; "Domestic Interior," *Outside History, New York*, W.W. Norton, 1990.

Lucille Clifton; "Far Memory, 7 Gloria Mundi," *The Book of Light*, Port Townsend, WA, Copper Canyon Press, 1993

Alicia Ostriker; *The Nakedness of the Fathers: Biblical Visions and Revisions*. New Brunswick, NJ: Rutgers University Press, 1994.

Library of Congress Cataloging-in-Publication Data

Kahn, Tamam.
Untold : a history of the wives of Prophet Muhammad / by Tamam Kahn.
    p. cm.
Includes bibliographical references.
ISBN 978-0-9823246-5-3 (alk. paper)
1. Muhammad, Prophet, d. 632--Family. I. Title.
BP76.8.K55 2010
297.6'42--dc22
                                    2010005893

Monkfish Book Publishing Company
27 Lamoree Road
Rhinebeck, New York 12572
USA 845-876-4861

for my wonderful husband, Shabda,
whose heartfelt encouragement made this book possible

and

for my great friend and editor Wendy Taylor Carlisle
whose keen intellect and persistence
brought these pages alive

CONTENTS

ACKNOWLEDGEMENTS

I would like to thank Fred Chappell for suggesting the master plan to incorporate research and poetry. I'm grateful to Dr. Arthur Buehler for his scholarly help and encouragement. This book would not have been possible without the brilliant editing of Wendy Taylor Carlisle, and the patience and support of my husband, Shabda Kahn. Thanks go to Wendy Garling, Matt Cohen and Rahim St John for additional editing and to Jelehla Ziemba, Samia Bloch, and Kyra Epstein for formatting. Appreciation to Paul Cohen for believing in this book, Georgia Dent for the beautiful cover design, and to Ruth Padel for the title.

Each of the following have contributed in some way to this venture, and so thanks are offered.

Sidi Ahmed Kostas, Najat Kostas, and the Sufi women of Marrakesh, Hadia Affronti, Amina Mousa, Laura Shelly, Imam Bilal Hyde, Faisal Muqaddam, Dr. Arif Jamal, Hamza El Din, Pir Zia Inayat Khan, Mirza Inayat Khan, Taj Inayat Khan, Jonathan Granoff, Moon Granoff, Daisy Khan, Dr. Nahid Angha and Dr. 'Ali Kianfar, Sheikh Ahmed Tijani, Khalifa 'Ali Ahmed Abul Fathi, Imam Medhi Khorasani, Sherif Baba, Tai Situpa, Saadi Douglas-Klotz, China Galland, Kabir Helminski, Nuha Abed, Todd Lapidus, Coleman Barks, Zuleikha, Naomi Shihab Nye, Marie Howe, Khalid Mattawa, Adonis, Jack Gilbert, Wendy Palmer, Ammon Haggerty, Solomon Kahn, Karim Baer, Dr. Farida 'Ali, Reza Aslan, Talat Halman, Shabda Owens, Arnold Kotler, Mirabai Starr, Sarah Morgan, Asha Greer, David Carlisle, Sabura Meyer, Wali 'Ali Meyer, Paula Saffire, Shahabuddin Less, Kothreneda Less, Khadija Goforth, Shakina Reinhertz, Irina Mikhailova, Aziz Abbatiello, Eva Latifa Cristofalo, Hilal Sala, Amrita Blaine, Dilwara Fletcher, Fadhilla Bradley, Toni Minnecola, Jonathan Iqbal Lewis, Sherry Ruth Anderson, Palden Alioto, Gayan Long, Allaudin Mathieu, 'A'isha Gray Henry, and many others.

FOREWORD

Untold: A History of the Wives of Prophet Muhammad is composed in a literary form called "prosimetrum" which alternates sections of prose with poems. This form has a long history in both Eastern and Western literatures and the Arabic *qasidat al-nathra* is closely related to it. The best known example in Western literature is probably *The Consolation of Philosophy* by Boethius, written ca. 522 CE by a jailed schoolmaster awaiting execution. It has provided thousands upon thousands with hope and comfort.

In that work, as in this present one, the narrative and expository elements are outlined in prose while the more personal and dramatic material is rendered in songs. Lyric poetry aims at the most concentrated, vivid, and economical expressions and so is not well suited to detailing the temporal progress of long and involved historical episodes. The lyric is, above all, *immediate* in its portrayals of situations, moods, states of mind, facets of character, and climactic moments so it must distill its materials in short, separate bursts of time. Sequential narrative and logical development are better fitted to the more relaxed movement of prose.

Reading through "Untold" is like making a journey through a broad, colorful, desert landscape as one is carried along in prose and then being halted by sudden encounters with personages who eagerly tell their stories or by striking features of landscape that offer themes and images for meditation. When the journey provides understanding, the abrupt bursts of poetry offer exhilaration. Each form is indispensable to the other.

Fred Chappell

Author of *Shadow Box* and *I am One of You Forever*

who do you think you are?

Who said you could do this? Who
are your ancestors, professors, godparents,
your stewards of the seen and unseen?
Locate for us your committee of yes.
List your lectures, your papers, the degrees
which announce your right to write
about the Prophet's wives.
Who is your imam? Where is his mosque?
If you are unable to answer
a curious sister, who do you think you are,
imagining Khadija?

If there is no one to speak for you,
you must defend yourself.

I am a pilgrim, a pen with child's heart,
following the foremothers through
doors shut on centuries of stolen words, across
floors now hushed in Saudi cement, down
steps to the cellar filled with the *Hijaz* story-jars.
Unsealed, the jars open their mouths,
speak to me. I listen.

I splash water on my face,
as Khadija did. Sometimes I speak
as harshly as Hafsa. I ask
forgiveness, in the way of 'A'isha.
Far from the Great River of my birth,
as Mariya was from hers,
in Zaynab's wake, I swim amid
the Names of God. Like each
of these women, I touch
my forehead to the ground and say:
no god but God.

I am here with a message:
Conversation with these women
will never end.

Hijaz — Western Arabian Peninsula, includes Mecca and Medina.

PREFACE

Marrakesh

I N JUNE 1998, I knocked on the door of an apartment in Marrakesh, and my life changed. My husband, Shabda, and I had just finished leading a group to the Sacred Music Festival in Fez, Morocco. We were spending a week in Marrakesh and I asked to be included in a Sufi women's chanting session (*dhikr*). The next day, I was given an address, and told to be there at five o'clock. Moroccan Sufis are publicly quiet about their path, but when the door sprang open on the apartment of the Sufi group, I was greeted by shouts of praise God (*al-hamdu l'illah!*) and fierce, enthusiastic hugs. All around me were women in bright robes (*djelabas*) speaking in French, or Arabic. I replied in my halting French, swept up by intense female energy.

The room I entered was in the home of three Sufi sisters. Along the walls were brocade-cushioned benches; in the middle of the room, children played. In this place, set aside for women's practice, curious faces surrounded me. After I was introduced, we began to chant. Amazed and energized, I connected with my breath, heart, and gut, with these women's deep reserves of power and devotion.

Verses from the Qur'an, songs, names of God — these women were chanting athletes. When the hour came for silent dhikr, our fingers sped around two prayer beads (*tasbihs*) one held in either hand — a moment with each bead, a spiritual formula tasted in the mouth, sometimes a sound, sometimes a word "spoken by the heart," only occasionally bursts of leh-leh-leh-leh! We were traveling at the speed of light, or so it seemed. As the poet Rumi affirms, "We break the wineglass, and fall toward the glassblower's breath."[1] Four hours later, feeling as if no time had passed, I was back in our hotel.

Days later, I found myself at the sister's home again; this time the sisters told me I was to receive a henna gift. When I asked why, the eldest sister said — "because it makes us happy."

heart not dog (*qalb not kalb*)

How long have you been with us? All my life
I tell them, but I'm never believed.
                              — Khaled Mattawa, *Libyan-American poet*

Here is my skin
for your happiness,
Marrakesh women.
Here are my open palms,
my tanned feet. Here
I am, a scrubbed-clean surface for
Zera-with-the-kohl-rimmed-eyes,
the artist who pens loops and trellises
in henna, the color of raisins.

You say, don't move. The hours pass.
The pattern spreads. No cell phone, no translator,
I can't move. You dressed me.
I wear your silver and green
robe from Mecca;
I mix up the Arabic, swap dog for heart.
You're laughing;
you're sister-ing me;
one of you lifts a glass of mint tea
to my lips. It's clear now.
You've marked me
with a henna homing device,
a tag in case I'm far away — or ever lost.

During that long evening, my husband twice sent a car for me. Once, they sent it back. At midnight they released me. When I returned to California two days later, I walked into my upscale clothing store with feet and hands still tattooed in brown lace.

Someone asked what happened. I discovered it was hard to talk about. I began to read recent biographies of Prophet Muhammad, first the one by Karen Armstrong, then by Martin Lings. I was fascinated. The women described there, wives and daughters of the Prophet — did they have the fierce, elegant energy I found at the *dhikr*? Did they possess the same strength I saw in those Moroccan mothers, daughters and sisters, the same ardor, the same discipline?

A thousand and one nights

When I was old enough to sit for most of a story, my father would read to me at bedtime from his boyhood book of *The Arabian Nights,* with "Merry Christmas, for John from Louise" handwritten on the first page. Slipped inside, was a card with my father's name and a smeared imprint: "The Hill School." The card was embellished with three metallic stars. The book did not list an author's name, only the illustrator's. Inside, on tea-colored pages, his strange and compelling pictures drew me into an exotic world that blended Art Deco with classic Middle-Eastern images of minarets and keyhole doors and camels.

My father was an attorney who loved history and had a mystic bias. He wrote his senior thesis at Princeton on "Mysticism as Proof of the Existence of God." I grew up surrounded by Sir Richard Burton's Aladdin and 'Ali Baba. Shaharazad of the *Thousand and One Nights*, instructed me in fairness and bravery. These fables linked enchanted Arabia with my Midwestern America. I was brought up to feel anything was possible for a bright, curious girl. Stories of clever desert women confirmed my belief.

In 'Ali Baba and the Forty Robbers," I was especially drawn to Morgiana (an anglicized version of Mughiana) the beautiful young servant who saves 'Ali Baba and wins her freedom, all by means of clear thinking:

reading the Arabian Nights

In a town in Persia there lived two brothers,
Papa began,
both of us pulled thread by thread
into the tapestry of a thousand nights.

It was *'Ali Baba* again, with that slave-girl
in bangles and flowing skirts.
I asked him: How did that girl know the way
to kill? Where would she get the strength

to pour hot oil into the thirty-nine enormous jars?
How did she find the thief? Each night
I slept in the whisper of new words:
caliph and Persia, Aladdin and *Badr al-Budur* —

moon of moons. Shaharazad
used tales to tame a sultan. I turned
toward the desert each night as the Midwest sky
inked in and Papa called up an escape

from sand-less lives. My father turned the pages.
I craned my neck to see each picture,
longed to find a home
that did not vanish into *jinn* smoke.

Below one illustration of Aladdin
speaking to the genie, the caption read:
I am hungry, bring me something to eat.
When things were good, the earringed giant

brought the boy a silver tray:
twelve plates of cracked lamb and mint,
sweet cakes, chopped figs with cream;
all from his towering cloud. And then

the magus came along to steal a boy's good fortune,
with the cry: *new lamps for old.* But Papa would read on
until the sandy world rang right again.
Held as I was in a child's life, I learned

open sesame! That year, Papa mastered
the trick of blowing a dime
from the table top into a glass.
You need to believe you can, **he said,** *and practice.*

In the late sixties I was a college sophomore at Sarah Lawrence. My advisor
was the brilliant Adda Bozeman. In her World Politics and Culture class,
I uncovered the modern Middle East; I devoured the few books on Islam
available in English. I went to the new mosque in Washington; I spoke to
an imam; I wrote a paper titled "Arabic Literature in Translation," but Islam
remained a mystery to me.

Eight years later in California, I heard The Sufi Choir, the musical expression of American Chishti Sufis. Through them I came to know my
future husband, the musician Shabda Kahn. He grew up in New York, the
son of German Jewish immigrants and had become part of the universal
Sufi lineage of the Indian mystic, Hazrat Inayat Khan, whose message was
one of "love, harmony, and beauty."

The Sufi sees the one truth in all forms… Its central theme is to produce consciousness of the divinity of the human soul; and toward this end, the Sufi teaching is given.

Sufism has …always been considered as the essence of every religion and all religions. Thus when it was given to the world of Islam, it was presented by the great Sufis in Muslim terminology… The God of the Sufi is the God of all, [one's] very being.[2]

This teaching, known as "the Message of our time," spoke to me.

Shabda and I married and moved into a house near San Francisco called "The Garden of Allah" with students of his deceased American teacher, Samuel L. Lewis. I began to study and found the American Chishti path inclusive. I learned traditional Sufism in most of the world is the path of mysticism within Islam. We began to meet other Sufis, a teacher (*murshid*) from Jordan, the Mevlevi whirling practitioners (*dervishes*), and a Moroccan spiritual guide (*muqaddam*). We became teachers and group leaders; we traveled to the Middle East and I was finally able to see minarets, a keyhole door, working camels.

Mawlud and the treasure

The year after my experience in Marrakesh, my husband and I traveled again to Morocco, this time to Oujda on the Algerian border, to a celebration commemorating the birth of Prophet Muhammad (*Milad an-nabi*), celebrated on the full moon and called by Moroccans "*Mawlud.*"

at the Zaki Hotel
for Amina M.

Seems the heat that glazed the bus roof, jiggled
the landscape as we drove east —

that heat is gone. Gone too are boundaries or the need for them.
Awake in deep night, my windows open

to the highway, I hear a guard outside, a small sound.
"Try sleep," clicks the clock. The ceiling's vanished.

We pilgrims, a field of sleep on 33 mattresses
cover ourselves with a fat white moon.

"Let the night, o, let the night!"
I hear it everywhere in this ferocity of shine.

On the western edge of Morocco, the King is going
to bed after *Mawlud dhikr*; he removes

the pale *djelaba*, the scarlet cap, sets down
the wooden beads with the blue woven cord. In 27 days

his heart will stop.
Allah, Allah, Allah, repeat the stars.

He's moving bead by bead toward the time when the kingdom
will grieve and pull its borders close.

But tonight — in this perfect openness, we breathe
the absence of walls, the blessing in light.

We will be gone from here when the *Mawlud* is done,
when the moon swells again inside his interruption, when

lions gather to keep watch between kings.

Mawlud. 2 a.m. Under the full moon, Sufi men gather outside in enormous tents. Inside, in 100-degree air, two thousand women jam into the mosque to celebrate the Prophet, his wives and daughters. These women chant their practice every day. All of them know the words to the song "Welcome to the Prophet." Some pass into ecstatic states. In their company, my reality melts. I take a step forward. Their power draws me in.

Inspired by my experiences in Morocco, the women there, and the stories I was discovering about the Prophet's family, I wrote a poem, drawing from both written sources and intuition. I imagined myself into Khadija's life. So this book began.

Just at this time a startling thing happened. My husband Shabda Kahn was appointed the spiritual guide (*pir*) of the Sufi Ruhaniat International. His gift of responsibility deepened my own commitment to spiritual practice. From these experiences came the poems and stories through which I reached into the cave in my life where the treasure lay.

the zikr room on Norwich Street

I

The room with
the tall lamp
the blur of beads across my hands...
the chanting lips: *Allah, Allah,*
the couch
the mind blinded; the heart —
the tremendous tent which holds a throng.

II

Inside the tent, where Khadija sits
so plain and fine, she gives me
what I need, but I don't know this now.

'A'isha looks like my girlhood
friend. Her laugh
lights each unasked question as if it were a sparkler.

Zaynab watches me
like she knows just where I'd go
if I were the road and she the constant yellow line.

Fatima stirs the water
with a stick. Her look
arouses oceans. I dive,
and dive again then towel-down in the room.

III

The room with
the tall lamp,
the blur of beads across my hands...
the chanting lips *Allah, Allah,*
the couch, the steaming cup of tea
and now for history.

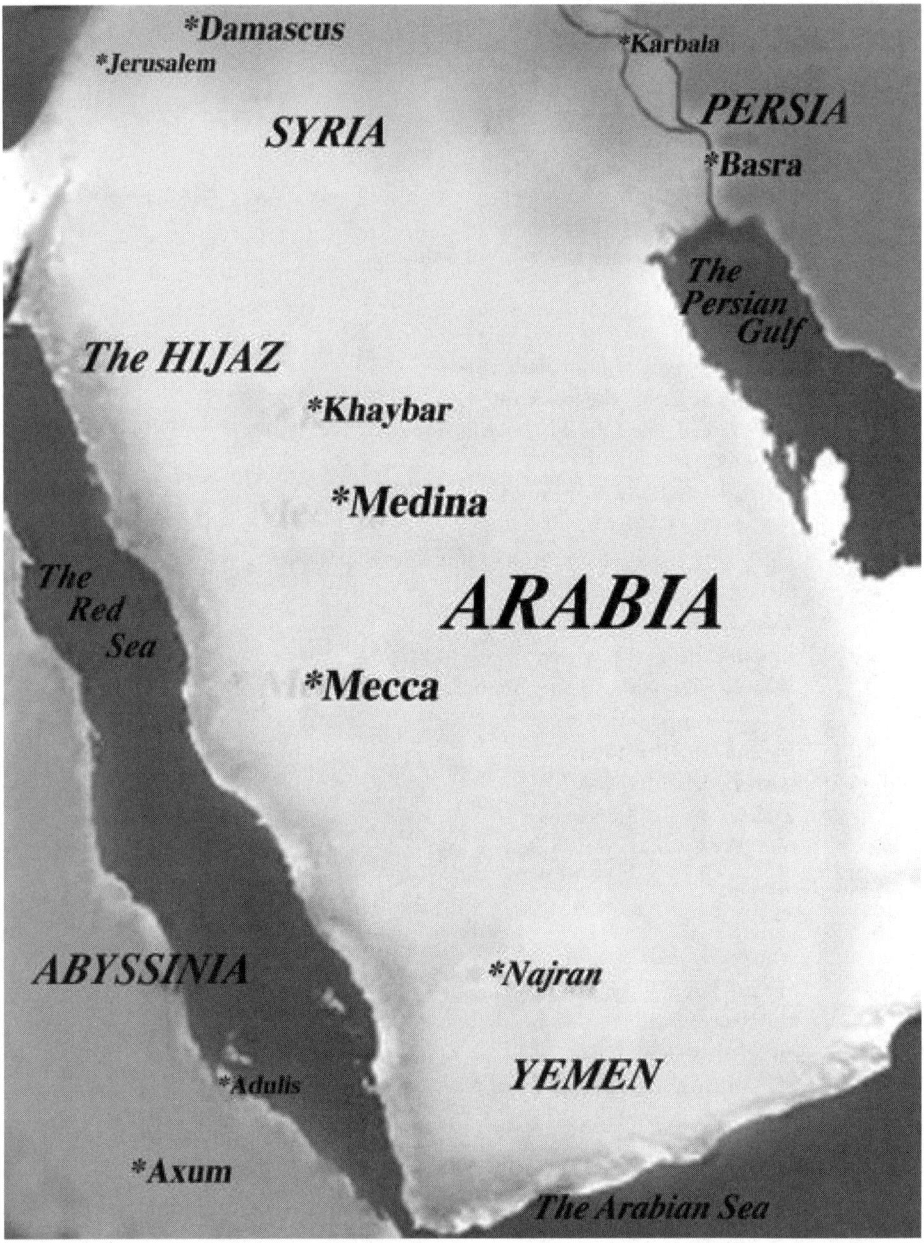
*Damascus
*Jerusalem
*Karbala
SYRIA
PERSIA
*Basra
The Persian Gulf
The HIJAZ
*Khaybar
*Medina
The Red Sea
ARABIA
*Mecca
ABYSSINIA
*Najran
YEMEN
*Adulis
*Axum
The Arabian Sea

INTRODUCTION

DESPITE THE IMPORTANCE of the first Muslim women, few people in the non-Islamic world know their names. We have heard of Omar Khayaam. We are familiar with the story of Shaharazad, a fanciful tale combining legends from Persia, Arabia, Turkey, and India. Such a fable is very distant from the hadith, the collected sayings and actions of Muhammad written in narrative form and traced to an authenticated source.[3] This material (the hadith) must be transmitted by someone in the line of "tellers" called "the chain" (*isnad*), and passed on exactly as he or she was first told. In Islamic literature, prose can be interspersed with poetry. But in the hadith literature, the tradition is to use only the hadith — with no embellishment — because the purpose of the hadith collections is to prevent embellishment which explains why there are few modern poems about the Mothers of Islam. Traditionally, a Muslim writer would not be inclined to discuss Khadija's feelings, as I have done.

Before writing about these women, I read every biography I could find in English, becoming familiar with their culture through study of Arabic, the Qur'an, hadith, and other secondary literature. I learned from and was inspired by all manner of scholarship. I worked toward primary sources. I was amazed at the lack of information, especially in English, and the holes in the research. Disagreements among scholars convinced me of the notion that all history is somewhat accurate and somewhat fictitious. Often the trail seemed cold and then another treasure would appear. I was happy to find the name of the Christian city in Ethiopia — Aksum (Axum) — which gave Muhammad's earliest followers asylum. Information accumulated. Soon I began to write about these women, opening their lives through my poetry, linking the historical and the intuitive as respectfully as possible.

There is a term for the time before Islam that is often misunderstood. *Jahiliyya* is known as the "Era of Ignorance," although brutality, arrogance, and retaliation are more faithful to the Arabic. Muhammad's approach was one of gentleness, discernment, calm deliberation known as *hilm*, an attribute of Allah (*Ya-Halim*), as well as an antidote to this kind of attitude and behavior:

9

instructions for *Jahiliyya*

...the jahil, *a wild, violent and impetuous character who follows*
the inspiration of unbridled passion and is cruel by following his
animal instincts; in one word, a barbarian.

— Ignaz Goldziher

Know you are right.
Think fist and knife-edge.
Do not appear
foolish, no matter what.

Control your woman
and your guests; keep them
a little afraid, and thankful
for your protection.

Guard your clan's
honor. Carve a notch
on your weapon of choice
for each successful payback.

If someone calls you animal,
smile and answer — lion,
hyena, crocodile, fighting cock—
the meek are the pack animals of the ferocious.[4]

Many women in pre-Islamic time suffered under this attitude. In a world best described as "primitive," women were marginalized and unequal, used for enjoyment and breeding. Girl infants were sometimes buried alive; women had no property or dowry rights; widows were left as chattel to the male heirs of a deceased husband. Survival for most women meant being attached to a family unit. Compared to the privilege of men, women's lot appeared to be no better than slavery.

But as I studied further, I discovered that even during this time before Islam, a parallel matriarchic culture existed in parts of Arabia. Muhammad's mother, Amina, stayed with her clan to give birth to her baby, as was the custom in matriarchies, and remained with them until she died when the boy was seven. The hadith spoke of Salama, mother of the Prophet's grandfather, "[B]ecause of her noble birth and her high position among her people, [she] never allowed herself to marry anyone except under the condition that she would be her own master and retain the initiative to leave her husband if she disliked him."[5] Her son, 'Abd al-Mutalib, raised Muhammad after Amina died. Khadija, the Prophet's wife, as a very wealthy widow, ran her own business. These were women with authority. The referent material, which makes up the Islamic canon, was written down at a time when the patrilineal system had overridden the matrilineal, so that much information about descent through the mother was lost or considered secondary at best.

With the rise of Islam, privileged women lost certain freedoms, but much of what Muhammad brought to seventh-century Arabian culture benefited women. Revelation, which became what is known as the Qur'an, was the new lawmaker as well as inspirer and teacher. It is important to understand how Revelation differed from normal speech in Muhammad's mouth. He would faint or begin to sweat and tremble and then talk in an elegant speaking voice — unlike his own — with the most beautiful phrases that often caused the listener to remember every word, as if engraved in his or her heart. Those words were repeated, and later gathered into the Qur'an. Revelation specified every woman had the right to inherit her husband's property and to use her own dowry as she wished. If divorced, she could take her dowry with her. Although Muhammad was married to multiple women at the time this verse was spoken, the Qur'an stated that monogamy was the preferred form of marriage, but to ensure that widows and single women were cared for, a man could have four wives if he treated them equally. ...[M]arry from among women such as are lawful to you — two, or three, or four; but if you have reason to fear that you might not treat them with equal fairness, then only one...[Q. 4:3].

Muhammad felt strongly about women's equality. It may seem to us that women's rights declined during Muhammad's time, but the Qur'an outlines many rights for women. These rules for women's rights may seem small, but they were seen as outrageous, privileged precedent. According to the Qur'an, for instance, a woman may inherit half of what her brothers receive. Seen in context, this balances out, since her family's men are required to provide the bridal money. Also, women's witness is accepted in the law stated by the Qur'an, even though it is worth half of that of a man.

Muhammad knew a great deal about marriage. He understood it as a sacred container for love and family, but also as an effective tool to forge difficult alliances. He was exclusively with his first wife, Khadija, for twenty-five years. He married two of their daughters, Ruqayya and Umm Kulthum to his companion 'Uthman, of the difficult and powerful Umayyan family, and later chose Umm Habiba, a Umayyan, for his own wife. The union between Mariya and Muhammad made the people of Egypt part of the family. He had two Jewish wives, Rayhana and Safiyya. Juwayriyya saved her entire people from slavery by becoming Muhammad's wife. Matrimony rescued widows and was a kind of peace plan.

Muhammad listened to women and sought their opinions. His wife, Umm Salama, inquired about Revelation's lack of references to women. Soon after, the Messenger was moved to recite this verse which included women. These words made clear the equality of all believers and became known as Umm Salama's verse: ...*[A]ll men and women who are patient in adversity, and all men and women who humble themselves and all men and women who give in charity... and all men and women who remember God unceaseingly; for them has God readied forgiveness of sins and a mighty reward.* [Q. 33:35].

"The verse of the curtain" appeared later, under circumstances associated with expansion of the community. At this time the Prophet lived in a communal house next to the mosque. Because he was becoming famous, the attractive women of his household suffered from scrutiny by the men he advised. God's Words, revealed on the night of the wedding of the Prophet and Zaynab b. Jahsh, designated a curtain — not a veil — be dropped between male strangers and the Prophet's wives. *And whenever you ask them for anything that you need, ask them from behind a screen. This will deepen the purity of your hearts and theirs.* [Q. 33:53]. In another verse, the women of the community around Muhammad (*umma*) were asked to cover themselves with extra cloth when out of doors to signify their prestige as well as offer them protection. ...*[T]hey should draw over themselves some of their outer garments: this will be more conducive to their being recognized and not annoyed.* [Q. 24:31, 33:59]. In this way, the female companions became their own community.

Real isolation of women began with the Prophet's death. Two years later the caliph 'Umar, while trying to preserve what he believed to be Islam, attempted to isolate women in their homes and bar them from the mosque. Failing that, he introduced segregated prayer and arranged that only men could be teachers and religious leaders. During a speech in Medina twelve years after Muhammad's death, 'Umar maintained wrongly that the stoning of women accused of adultery was part of the Qur'an.[6] Thus began the reversals in social reforms. The decline of women's rights was assisted by the reading of hadith that reflected an intentional patriarchal slant.

Under the Prophet's successors, the empowerment of women gradually ceased. The clouds of the *jahiliyya* attitude obscured Muhammad's valued words and actions, which had lifted the women around him and let them shine. And hadn't the first wife, Khadija, raised her husband up, supporting him in every way? Yet much of the popular culture of Islamic tradition oppressed women then and now. The limits of today's speech, dress and habits adopted in the name of the customs of the Prophet (*sunna*) make historical biography such as this book challenging. Can we stay open-minded to who these lively women might have been? Can we relax and let the poetry of their lives sing to us?

galaxies

for Sidi Ahmed

The desert stretches skyward.
Evening rolls down the sequence
of color to black.
Out past the tents, the *faqiri* moon,
a rim-slip of silver, sets.

Now the milky-way is everything —
Glisten is flung from there, out of the pools
of paradise where the *Mothers of Islam* bathe:

Amina, and Halima — the-wet-nurse
are first with splash and laughter;
then wives: Khadija and 'A'isha;
Umm Habiba, Umm Salama, Sawda, Hafsa, Rayhana,
Safiyya, Mariya, Zaynab, Juwayriyya. and Maymuna —
daughters: Zaynab, Ruqayya, Umm Kulthum and Fatima.
A shower of blessings to all!

Honored by the Prophet, each woman
a galaxy, a night breeze, a mysterious pearl;
each one a solar system, complete in the white
blaze of her name. They lighten the sky,
beauty-mark the heavens, and heighten my astonishment
until I'm milk-marked and speechless. They say:
        Those earthly years

we ringed 'round him,
held everything firm, as tent pegs do,
we kept him love-heavy;

husband, father, light-of-a-life-time.
We star in a thousand family stories.
                                    Write them.

KHADIJA, THE WHITE SHADE CLOUD

...Home is a sleeping child,
an open mind

and our effects,
shrugged and settled
in the sort of light
jugs and kettles
grow important by.

Eavan Boland, *Domestic Interior*

Khadija, the White Shade Cloud

K HADIJA'S IMPRINT ON the world of Islam has not faded over the centuries. In that world she is universally loved and appreciated. Yet if she knew what had been made of her life, she might be astonished at the growth of myth and idealization. She'd smile at being called *glorious*, *pure*, and *perfect*. Beneath flowery phrases about Khadija, a real woman stretches and moves, a person with a remarkable life from the time way before Islam became a world religion.

Khadija's life began in Mecca, fifty miles from the Red Sea, surrounded by bare mountains. There she must have drunk from the well of *Zamzam*, visited the shrine of the *Ka'ba* and rested her hand on the cornerstone — the black meteorite — some fourteen hundred years ago. As this sacred stone became the ritual center of the Muslim world, Khadija can be seen as the rock upon which Muhammad built his family and religion. She was his first and only wife for twenty-five years. She was an unveiled woman, a matriarch, a mother and a wealthy and successful businesswoman.

The well-known quotation from hadith, "Cover me, cover me!" gives a clear window into her first moments as wife of a Prophet. It began the day Muhammad fled a cave on Mount Hira right after his harrowing experience when he was grasped and commanded to speak by an insistent Angel Gabriel — a story that marks the beginning of Revelation. Muhammad rushed to Khadija for protection.

Khadija

He said,
> Cover me
> I can't bear what I've seen and heard.

She said,
> Hush! You are safe now.

He said nothing.

She said, rocking him,
> I am womb-rooted, and sure.
> Tell me.

He said nothing for a long time.

Then he said,
>I was squeezed and forced to recite.
>A terrifying being filled the sky
>told me, You are God's Prophet and I am Gabriel.

She said nothing.

Then she said,
>The power of His language in your unschooled mouth
>will bring your camel to her knees
>and much of the world.
>These verses you speak will be repeated
>for more than a thousand years.
>This I know.

Look to your heart.

Her capacity to hold a calm and insightful attitude allowed Khadija to "cover" her husband and help him return to his senses at the moment of enormous crisis. Starting that day, this practical woman would need to balance everyday life with Divine Reality — God's Message streaming through her husband. Could she have imagined such a life?

Hadith tells of an early incident hinting about future partnership and prophesy. Picture a spring day in Arabia. The Meccan mothers have taken their daughters, as their mothers did before them, to a shrine not far from Mecca to honor a family deity. It is a formal ritual, and the young girl, Khadija, is sitting by her sister and cousins, listening to the chanting. She is wearing a new honey-colored dress from Syria. She daydreams.

the visitor

On the women's sacred day, a man
appeared. I didn't see him, fixed as I was
on the gibberish of cricket, insect clack and buzz.
Later my cousin swore he was a jinn,
a wraith whose phantom glance inhaled us,
or perhaps she said, a swirl of wind
who whirled the petals of us like the ones
we'd strewn across al-'Uzza's shrine. He must
have scattered everything: the plates, the coins —
and no one heard his words but me. He uttered
the puzzle that I would solve when I was grown:

Ahmad the Messenger of God transmits His Word.
Let any girl who wants to marry him — do so.
I sat alone. The others fumbled for a stone to throw.

The hadith states that a God-intoxicated man (*majdhub*), at a shrine during a religious festival, yelled out a message meant for Khadija about marrying God's Messenger.[7] He used the name *Ahmad,* which is another name for Muhammad, who may not have been born when this prophecy happened. Most were disturbed, but the commentator notes that Khadija stayed calm.

There is a record of seven generations (including Khadija), her mother, Fatima, the daughter of (*bint or b.)* Zayda, her grandmother, and so forth.[8] This lengthy record would indicate a strong matriarchal line and a good chance that these women worshiped at a shrine to one of the three famous goddesses. It may be that the girls and women visited the shrine at Nakhlah, sacred to the divine mediator, al-'Uzza since her great-great-grandmother's name was Atiqa b. 'Abdul 'Uzza.

We know only a few bare facts about Khadija before she met the Prophet. Afterward she is never absent from the story of his life. To mention her name is to connect with the Prophet's matrix. She is part of all that is vivid in that landscape of dusty earth and enormous blue sky; the sustaining date fruit, the yellow clusters of the acacia (*talh)* tree. She is the underground river beneath desert palmaries and gardens.

Her father was Khuwaylid, a merchant who accumulated a large fortune by selling goods in Yemen and Syria. We do know that Khadija's business acumen was attested to and well known. Her father died sometime around 585, her mother sometime earlier. She inherited and managed a large fortune and, being an able manager, she did well. She was twice married and widowed. Khadija raised a boy and girl in those early marriages, yet history tells us nothing except their names.[9] She gave instructions to male workers and servants. Under her direction, her caravans engaged in trade from Syria to Yemen. There is no mention of her education, although she would have needed to read, write and have a basic understanding of mathematics. Profits were made. Well-born citizen, widow, mother — this young woman, living at the end of the sixth century walked through Mecca unveiled and respected. What would it be like to see her for a moment at the warehouse just after a shipment of goods arrived?

brocade *(al-dibaja)*

for Sabura Rose

After the miles of squint-white desert,
after the bundles were pulled
from the camels, and heaped on
her warehouse floor,

Khadija's blade —
lit by a shaft of granular sunlight from the ceiling grid —
flashes as she bends
to slit the sack, the Damascus pack
with the red wax seal.

In a hush of Phoenician burlap:
folded enchantment,
pearly Sassanian silks, textile messengers
fluent in Arabic, defining *dibaja* —
as "elegance," and "brocade."

But this was a made-up story. Instead,
let her kneel, cut the bag open,
place the knife by the ledger, and lift
each tunic — plain, well-made;
examine the cloth quickly
with practiced eye and hand,

her damp face beautiful in its concentration.

Years afterward, Muhammad, then known as *Amin the Trustworthy*, was hired by Khadija to take one of her caravans to Syria. A servant went along. When the caravan returned he told Khadija the story of Muhammad and a Christian monk. The monk had approached Muhammad, who was seated beneath a tree. Awestruck, he said, "None other than a prophet sits beneath this tree." This story combined with the financial windfall from sales of her goods stirred Khadija's interest in the young man. She sent for him, for on his own, he could never have approached the successful, sought-after woman. Although his parents had been prominent, he was an orphan; with no social standing.[10] She spoke to him: "…your kinship to me, your standing among your people, your reliability, good character, and truthfulness make you a desired match." In this way, the widowed Khadija chose Muhammad as her next husband, a proposal he gladly accepted.

Muhammad comes to collect his salary

This is how history begins: lightning,
a shawl of cloud, perfume.

Fresh split
and burning like a green date-palm,
Khadija waits in the wood smoke
as if grazed by lightning. The man is
standing before her, she sees him
outlined by a white and blue alphabet.

He says, "good morning,"
she waits as the Names to open, to hear them
cool the air:

Amin. Ahmad. Hamid. Mahmud,
Rahmat al-'alamin
Muhammad, the Mercy to the Worlds —

The man is speaking.
He waits quietly for her reply.

Khadija! Answer him. Love him well.
You will be to him the one white shade cloud overhead at noon.

Khadija places the silver coins in the *hudah's* hand.

Her fingers quiver, he notices that
she smells delicious and faintly of smoke.

Khadija, older and more experienced, guided her husband through the complex business and domestic relationships his new status as part of a household with servants, property, and influence entailed. All he needed to know about a woman's heart and the responsibilities of fatherhood he learned from her. From 595 until her death in 619, Khadija was his first and only wife. During the years of their marriage, Muhammad had several roles: from "the Trustworthy," to successful merchant, to the shocked recipient of Revelation, to the herald of God's Word, to *the Seal of the Prophets of the Book*. As his life evolved, Khadija's life changed drastically as well. She went from needing nothing to having nothing, not even daily food and water, or the freedom to leave the house — but that came later.

The Family

It appears the young Muhammad was twenty-five when he married, his wife was said to be forty, but it is likely she was younger.[11] The couple lived in Mecca and had a family, the only children he fathered except for a son born much later. The eldest was a son, Qasim, who died before his second birthday. There may have been another boy, 'Abdullah, who died right after his birth. The hadith are inconsistent. Then came four daughters: Zaynab, Ruqayya, Umm Kulthum, and Fatima.[12] Fatima outlived her parents and siblings.

The family was well liked and admired. There were servants and caravans that carried olives, jugs of their pressed oil — which burned in all the lamps — grain and oranges, fragrance and rare fabrics. Khadija wore a beautiful onyx necklace. The windows may have been set with tinted glass from Yemen. The family must have owned horses and camels and could afford to be generous to those less fortunate. What happened to the early years? No one kept a record of that time. Of the later years there is a smattering of words, often about marriage and burial. The three daughters, at a young age, were promised to families liked by Khadija and Muhammad. By the time they were marriageable, none of the boys' parents approved of the family. Zaynab, the eldest had managed to marry anyway, but her sisters' weddings were canceled. 'Uthman, close friend of Muhammad, later married Ruqayya, then much later, her sister Umm Kulthum.

Umm Kulthum, third daughter

All of Khadija's daughters lived long enough to leave Mecca for exile in Medina. But the information about these three is spare, especially regarding Umm Kulthum.

Umm Kulthum: "mother-of-the-round-faced-one"

A round-faced one claimed you
as her mother; childless as you were.
Or so the Arabic says.
I looked you up,
and found statistics, dates and years
and categories: *The four daughters were*
and then your names
Zaynab, Ruqayya, Umm Kulthum and Fatima.

I read about your life, a canceled wedding day
and why? It was for politics.
a later marriage to 'Uthman — more politics;
and tears. Muhammad's,
when he sat upon your grave.
I found the clothing you wore —
the hadith from Anas read:
she wore a striped, silk cloak,
but he forgot to say the color
or occasion. Wedding? Hajj?

I'll never know. I closed my books.
I wondered why the *Rasul's* daughter
lived a spare and pallid life.
You might have spoken with
those who bowed to statues
and invoked the One God
with your mesmerizing words.
Perhaps you were silenced later
by writers with an ax to grind.
I like to think you clever,
drawing up a profile cloaked and cryptic:

Listen! Aside from mentioning
the Daughters of Muhammad,
no one speaks of Umm Kulthum.

What did she say or do? Little is offered but her strange name, which means literally, "mother of the round-faced one." But this name is not descriptive. Was she named after a close relative or friend? Apparently, she never had a child while she was married to 'Uthman, her father's close companion and a man who was happily married to her sister Ruqayya until he was widowed. Her father and husband were both away when Umm Kulthum died.

Ruqayya, second daughter

Ruqayya was one of the most beautiful women of her generation throughout all Mecca; and 'Uthman was a remarkably handsome man. He was married to a woman named Ramla, while married to Ruqayya then Umm Kulthum, but little is said about this.[13] Since Ruqayya and 'Uthman followed Muhammad, they were in constant danger from the aggressive Meccan establishment. Ultimately, they fled to Abyssinia, on the other side of the Red Sea. There, Ruqayya gave birth to a son, 'Abdullah. This child must have been a joy to both Khadija and Muhammad. He was the first grandson, as well as a bridge between the long-feuding clans, the Umayya ('Uthman) and the Hashim (Ruqayya). In those days, marriage was often a kind of peace treaty and a child could mean an end to aggression.[14]

'Abdullah, the child who brought peace, died tragically. It was said that a cock pecked his face or his eye and that Ruqayya was unable to stop the terrible inflammation that followed the wound. Given the especially painful circumstance, news of the child's death must have been devastating to his parents and his grandparents.

At that time, Ruqayya and 'Uthman were in exile in what is today Ethiopia. Could there have been cockfighting? One can imagine a circle of men and boys, shouting and betting, tossing coins into the circle.

Ruqayya, wakened by the words

And the winged one will appear and take him!

'Abdullah, small
beside the other boys,
has joined the men encircling
the fighting cocks.

His mother can imagine
how those birds strut and squawk,
and how a child might bend to look;
but what she cannot dream is
claws, the beak, his bloody face,
the soft cheeks torn, and then his eyes.

And the winged one will appear and take him!

Ruqayya runs to him, her only child—
who just this morning caught a butterfly
of iridescent green—
her blood-blind boy, stem-holder,
come to bind the clans. What happens next
flies in the face of all her dreams.
Battered, the boy 'Abdullah
sickens, dies, and writes in fire
on his mother's heart:

Death's Angel will appear and take him.

After the loss, they returned to Arabia and settled in Medina near Muham-mad, but that time was brief; Ruqayya, too, sickened and died, her husband at her side, while Muhammad fought the Battle of Badr. Soon after 'Uth-man married Umm Kulthum. Five years later and a decade after Khadija's death, perhaps seeking to enliven the link between 'Uthman's family and his, the Prophet married Umayya's great-granddaughter, Ramla, known as Umm Habiba. The marriage was childless, and after Muhammad's death the old enmities worsened to become the grudge that tore apart the Muslim world for centuries, as it does today. The early dream of a unified Islam may have died with 'Abdullah.

Zaynab, eldest daughter

Zaynab came to be separated from her husband, Abul-'As because he had sided with his family against Muhammad. The young couple loved each other, but Abul-'As lived in Mecca, and after awhile, sometime after Khadija died, Zaynab moved to Medina. This story begins after her husband's large caravan, returning from Syria, was captured by Muhammad's circle of fol-lowers known as the Companions. Abul-'As escaped and came to his wife's room under cover of night.

> **throw a lucky man in the sea, and he**
> **will come up with a fish in his mouth**
>
> *Arab proverb*

In the end he comes to her for good. But that night
he comes to her as a leaking cup, the outlaw
unable to hold both caravan and parental wishes;
all his luck, it seems, seeping out.
She hides him in her room behind the towels
and waits until the morning call to prayer.
She slips into the mosque
like sunlight through a young goat's ear.
The women smile and make room for her.

A shout! Zaynab cries out just before prayers:
"O people, I give protection to Abul-'As, the son of Rabi'."[15]
There, she's done it.
Muhammad spoke first after the Amen:
"Did you hear what I heard?"

And the women said yes!
Yes, we heard and we pray
your husband will be accepted, Zaynab,
because we are wed to the best and worst of ourselves,
the faithful and the unbeliever. We are both —
young couple, and prophetic
parent who decides what's best.

Then in the shocked silence, the long pause,
Muhammad speaks:

"Receive him with all honor…"

Imagine her running to Abul-'As and smoothing his hair,
pulling him to the mosque with caution-less joy.

Abul-'As went back to Mecca with his goods, and paid his debts. Then he left his parents and their religious beliefs to return to his wife as a follower of Muhammad.

Fatima, fourth daughter

If her elder sisters have been eclipsed by history, the youngest, Fatima, lived in the spotlight. The hadith offers collected stories of her childhood, marriage, family, and alliances. History has saved both her words and those of her father speaking to her. After Khadija's death, Muhammad leaned on her for support; later she was given the curious and weighty title, *Umm Abi-ha,* which translates as "the mother of her father." She became a symbol of protection in the culture of Islam. The open hand, a defining symbol of protection for Muslim women, is called "The Hand of Fatima." Fatima, her husband 'Ali, daughters Zaynab and Umm Kulthum, and her two sons, Hasan and Husayn, all survived the Prophet. Here is a version of the birth of this favored daughter. [16]

Khadija's lying-in

for Oona H.

Before the first cry, Khadija
knew that she would need
all the strength of her almost fifty
years to push the baby out.

My Syrian friend Nuha, told me this
in her perfect English. "And do you know
who delivered this child? The Women of the Book;
the sister of Moses, the Pharaoh's wife,
Abraham's spouse, and the Mother of Jesus;
Kulthum, Assiyya, Sarah, Mariam —
they brought her forth."
She spoke those names with ease,
the way you might say
any friend had come to help.
A Turkish elder spoke too of the birth
but named Hagar not Sarah. I say,
let them both be there. Let the chorus speak as one:

"Daughter of the Prophet, welcome! We come
to meet you at the door. In this life
you are the moon to your father's sun. We,
the welcoming blossom with many hands,
touch your head."

"Born into a flower," said her mother, Khadija.
And Fatima, called Zahra, came into that touch.

After the birth of Fatima, Muhammad's time for prophecy was approaching.
He began to seclude himself in nature. A family scene might have played
out with Khadija and the small child Fatima seeing Muhammad off on a
journey to the mountain:

seeing more

"It's late but everything comes next."
— Naomi Shihab Nye, *Jerusalem*

Fatima can't believe her eyes. Above the beekeeper
pulses a crown of bees. Signs are everywhere:
camel tracks, even the flies that trail them — iridescent.
Well water silvers like a splash of minnows
into every pail. No one seems to notice.
Her father's smile is whiter than his turban.
He straps on his pack and water skin, and lifts her
goodbye, then bends to set her down. He turns
to leave. "It's late. I have a long trek to the cave.
It will be dark soon. Be helpful to your mother."
She inhales in little sniffs

to keep his smell. She wants to run after him —
as if a dash of speed right then
might make him stay. She's staying put,
and watches his long shadow rubbed away
by light. His sandals twinkle, as if it's all a joke
on her, perception's trick. She grabs Khadija's hand.

"There's something with him, Mama.
Something that isn't us."

Revelation

What Fatima may have sensed was true; it reverberated with her father's experience with Revelation. In his fortieth year, during a month of retreat, when Muhammad was alone in a cave in Mount Hira, near Mecca, fasting and praying, Angel Gabriel appeared to him and asked him to recite. These were the first moments that the man, Muhammad, spoke God's Word. Hadith tells he fled to Khadija, in a state of apprehension, confusion, and profound fear. He believed he might have been taken over by a trickster, a disembodied entity (*jinn*). Khadija's Uncle Waraqa was the logical choice to advise Muhammad on what had happened to him. Waraqa was a mystic and a monotheist, some say a Christian. On hearing the tale, he believed that his niece's husband was the awaited Prophet. His words to Muhammad carried far-seeing reassurance and made him aware of his purpose in life.[17]

Khadija visits Uncle Waraqa

Out came my Uncle Waraqa, keen and vibrant, gesturing with his tall staff, saying twice, *Amin the Trustworthy, well, well.* I tried to say hello, but he was taking Muhammad's arm and pulling him into the house. *People of the Book have been whispering about this for years — you're the prophesied one. I can see it in your face. Your eyes are skylight. Your life just blew up. And what do you think of that, boy?* Muhammad just looked at him as if the old man were showing him rope tricks. He needed a lifeline, over the cliff as he was, and with a long drop beneath him. The rope circled over the uncle's head, he couldn't help but call out: *In God's name, throw me the rope!*

Uncle Waraqa laughed, *Just like Abraham and Noah, Moses and Jesus — your own people will call you a liar.* Muhammad, very pale, replied, *I'm losing my nerve, and need to know — just whom do I serve?* Waraqa looked at him hard and answered: *Let go.* And my husband awoke inside his own life.

Muhammad managed to live quietly for a while, raising his daughters and contemplating his work. But, when Revelation returned with insistence and commands, the spoken warnings appeared to challenge the belief systems at the center of Meccan culture. The famous square building, the *Ka'ba,* hosted the black stone and three hundred and sixty minor deities or "idols." It was believed to be founded — in this staggering view of human history — by "Prophet" Adam, and built by Abraham and Ishmael. It is theorized that twenty-seven hundred years before Muhammad's time, in the waning monotheistic Ishmaeli era: "No one left Mecca without carrying away with him a rock from the stones of the Sacred House as a token of reverence and as a sign of deep affection for Mecca. Wherever he settled he would erect that stone and circumambulate it in the same manner (as) the Ka'ba..."[18] This would help explain the gradual movement from One God to multiple deities. In the early seventh century Mecca's population included countless clans and ethnic groups. People from all over attended trade fairs in Mecca during the holy months, and paid homage to their own family gods. The notion of just One God, suggested by Muhammad, spelled out socioeconomic upheaval in Mecca. While Muhammad drew a loyal following he now had powerful enemies — a conservative majority that saw him as a madman and a threat to the status quo.

His message brought fear and insecurity to the traditionalists. Hostile locals hurled abuse at him, his family, and his followers. At this time Khadija no longer bought and sold goods but used her wealth to support the needs of the beleaguered group of companions and followers around her husband called the *umma.* Her relationship with the townspeople went from cordial hellos to taunts and slammed doors. Throughout these difficult times she remained dignified and kept the family together.

Khadija's hair

Talk to me Khadija.
I can't live up to what I say when
I speak the Word. I'm a simple man.
What am I to do?

> Leave the words to Allah
> and come down here. Let go
> your questions. You are truthful and good.
> That's enough. Come to bed.

It burns my bones —
the anger of my neighbors. Today
they tossed meat scraps on me
in the street. I feel unsure.

> Husband, look
> at a single hair from my head.
> It can split a stream of water
> and divide the wind.
> When the best of slaves surrenders doubt,
> God's music runs through him.
> Be a worthy slave.

A dumbstruck moon, their skin
in cool blue light, Muhammad
stands before his wife,
her long thick hair in his open palms.
Raising it to his eyes, he weeps.

Survival was difficult in the Arabian climate. Khadija gave birth to two or three children by former husbands and five by Muhammad, the last, Fatima, when she may have been past childbearing age. This was a wonder, but was only a small part of her activities. She was also Muhammad's closest confidant and the first practitioner of Islam, "a complete woman," in the true meaning of the term. History has only praise for her.

Early on, Allah's Messenger received guidance concerning *salat*, the Islamic ritual prayer performed five times daily. One story about this involves a man, Afif al-Kindi, who came to Mecca on a shopping trip. He stayed with Muhammad's uncle and while he was there he observed three people at the Ka'ba:

> He (Muhammad) faced the Ka'ba standing upright. A boy came and stood at his right. A woman soon came and stood behind them. The young man bowed. The boy and the woman bowed. The young man raised his head. The boy and the woman raised their heads. The young man went down in prostration. The boy and the woman went down in prostration. He told 'Abbas...(it was) amazing and... he later wished he had been their fourth.[19]

He was watching Muhammad, Khadija, and Muhammad's adopted nephew, 'Ali. The *salat* he witnessed is performed repeating *al-Fatiha*, the opening *sura* of the Qur'an. Khadija didn't hesitate to take up this ritual practice with the intention of becoming one with the One. Yet it is likely she continued to exemplify everyday life as a practice.

It was Khadija's job to run the household, directing her children, 'Ali, and the servants. She was also charged to separate Muhammad as much as possible from the enmity of his foes and the burdens of his public life; and to see to the momentary needs of the group—teaching, advising, supporting, and learning. Aging bodies grow stiff and painful. That is hard enough to accept, but to lose respect and money and be viewed as deluded by all but a handful of friends must have been very challenging.

During this time as well, the extended family was placed under a ban by the Quraysh, the all-powerful clan that ruled Mecca, from which, ironically, Muhammad was descended. Those of the Companions without protectors were sometimes taunted, beaten or killed.

No one was permitted to interact with them, marry them, or sell them any goods. They were not allowed to leave except for special holidays. The *umma* and their relatives all suffered hardship. Sanctions against them went on for nearly three years with great deprivation. To the Meccans, it was as if the belief of the Companions was a contagious disease. At great risk, friends sent a camel laden with supplies down the short road to their plain dwellings now and then, but it was an unreliable arrangement. The ban caused Khadija to suffer "house arrest" along with the others and her health was compromised by the food shortages.

the ban

The one gauze cloud
across the moon, the one woman,
thin and wrapped in fleece,
the one standing after her prayers,

the one asking *forgiveness*
for herself and her tormentors,
this one, Khadija, once
commanded Mecca with a glance,
now, the one starving
with her family, the one
banned from that extra splash of water
to wash the dust from her feet,
until the one drop of rain.
And then the next.

Khadija, who once had it all — wealth, honor, strength, grace, and a young husband — gave up everything for belief in Muhammad and a single Merciful God. Yet all the stories say she was calm, free of doubt, fearless and loving. The nourishment she gave to Muhammad was her willingness to turn her life upside down for him and for the Message spoken through him. But how does one survive, lit by proximity to a prophet, while faced with violent public disapproval and loss of status and fortune?

It is said that the words of Revelation that came from Muhammad's mouth sustained and guided her, as well as the community, through this dark time. The Qur'an is considered the miracle of Islam. There is something in Qur'anic Arabic that does not translate, especially into stiff English with Christian overtones. In fact, translations of the Qur'an are not considered to be the Qur'an at all.[20] Plainly, the multi-dimensional language nuances are inaccessible to those unfamiliar with Arabic.

It is awful to imagine this once-powerful matriarch of the family, Khadija, the beam of stability for Muhammad and the family of followers, slipping into an irreversible decline as Muhammad was coming into his life's work. When the Quraysh finally lifted the ban, there was a brief respite in enmity. The Prophet continued to be uncompromising in his principles, and civility gave way to more persecution and more danger for the Muslims.

In the year 619 Khadija died, at age 65 or younger. This painful loss was closely followed by the death of Abu Talib, the uncle who, as head of his clan, offered Muhammad protection, the man who loved him like a son. With the death of Khadija and his uncle, the cable holding Muhammad's life-as-he-knew-it was cut, and he was flung into an ocean of grief and caught up in a maelstrom of controversy and danger. Three years later he moved into exile in Medina and began a new life.

For centuries, the home where Khadija lived with the Messenger was honored. A ninth-century writer tells us: "Khadija's house at that time was the house still known today... Mu'awiya bought it and turned it into a mosque in which people could pray... The stone which is at the door to the left as you go in is the stone beneath which the Messenger of God used to sit to shelter himself when people threw stones at him..."[21]

Excavating Khadija's unknowable story from the ground that nurtures poetry may bring up many questions. Was Khadija optimistic or merely resigned? How did she balance the reality of her position with her practical nature? Let her pass from her life with her struggles peacefully resolved. Let her last room glow with the light she enters fearlessly, all traces of doubt and attachment gone. Let this luminosity be present in her physical body as she leaves earthly existence praying with certainty, "I witness — there is no Reality but God and I witness — Muhammad is the Prophet of God."

'A'ISHA, MATCHFIRE IN THE BACKLIGHT

...Before you know kindness as the deepest thing inside,
you must know sorrow as the other deepest thing
You must wake with sorrow.
You must speak to it till your voice
catches the thread of all sorrows
and you see the size of the cloth...

Naomi Shihab Nye, *Kindness*

'A'isha, matchfire in the backlight

IMAGINE 'A'ISHA ABANDONED in the desert, in the hills of stony sand, without a tree or building nearby. The sun inches up, climbing the terrible sky; 'A'isha stands stiff-backed, scanning the horizon until she collapses. The next thing she feels is the camel, his bristly muzzle pushing her. It startles the girl. The camel's young rider commands the beast to kneel.

> ### slander
>
> It began with that camel's lips
> worrying the cloth
> on my back, my foot
> grazed by the nose-rope,
> slack in the young rider's hand.
>
> How could such a simple rescue agitate
> the gossips? Thirty long days,
> rumors curdled the milk in my bowl
> The neighbors' words
> — *fitna, falatya*—
>
> were the signs that marked my place
> on a cold road where any woman
> shuffles when her husband
> gives her that flat stare. I wander there
> and wait for judgment
>
> until the Word comes down.

That morning early, fourteen-year old 'A'isha had wandered into the desert in search of a lost necklace, or perhaps to heed a call of nature, or because something out in the sand caught her eye. She was gone long enough for the caravan with her husband Muhammad and thirty or so of his companions to move off. Her camel with its curtained *howdah*, rose up to follow his brothers and she was so small, weighed so little that no one noticed her absence. Alone in the desert she waited for someone in the caravan to miss her, and come back to find her. She was almost lost to the dismaying heat and glare when a youth gave her water, helped her mount his camel and led her straight to her husband.

This is a joyful story. 'A'isha is safe, returned to her people without being harmed. Praise God. But as she rides into the encampment, her people respond coldly. She is the Prophet's wife, ill and weak with sun poisoning, so the story goes. Nevertheless the sight of her with an unrelated man is enough to set the camp troublemakers to whispering: Had she staged an encounter?

A negative view of women runs deep in the desert culture. It is commonly believed that woman, by her very nature, is pulled toward fornication. When Muhammad did not immediately stand up for his wife, as any wife might expect him to, she was stunned. She turned to her parents but they could do nothing. The camp hummed while Revelation offered nothing for nearly a month. 'A'isha protested her innocence. If she were pronounced guilty, the penalty would be terrible — divorce or possibly lifelong confinement. These punishments were a shadow, darkening the scene. Then Muhammad asked 'Ali his opinion. "O Messenger of God, Allah has placed no narrow limits on you. Many are the women like her. Examine her maid for the truth."[22]

'A'isha never forgave 'Ali for his words, even after she was cleared of all wrongdoing by Revelation [Q. 24:12]. Perhaps influenced by her ordeal, she studied law and learned the entire Qur'an by heart.

Before Widowhood

'A'isha was Muhammad's only virgin wife. She was betrothed to him while he was recovering from Khadija's death. The daughter of his close friend, Abu Bakr, she was married while still a child as was the custom, though her real marriage would not have been consummated until after she reached puberty. "...the Prophet dreamed that he saw a man who was carrying someone wrapped in a piece of silk. The man said to him, 'This is your wife, so uncover her.' The Prophet lifted the silk and there was 'A'isha." A few nights later he dreamed of an angel carrying the same bundle. Again it was 'A'isha.[23] It was literally a marriage made in heaven. In year one of the Muslim era the Prophet took Islam to Medina; 'A'isha followed with her father's family. Two years later she entered the Prophet's household. She was a special favorite, extremely bright and vivacious. Muhammad once told her she was dearer to him than butter with dates. She was also the woman at the Prophet's side when most Revelation descended. She recollects one such encounter between Muhammad and Gabriel:

> I saw Gabriel standing in my chamber. He was mounted on a horse and the Prophet of Allah was whispering to him. When the Prophet approached [me], I said, "O Messenger of Allah, who is that with whom I saw you whispering?" The Prophet replied, "You saw him?" I said that I had. He said, "Who does he look like?" I said, "Diyah al-Kalbi." The Prophet said, "What you saw is a great blessing. This is Gabriel." I hesitated until the Prophet said, "O 'A'isha, this is Gabriel who says, 'Peace be with you.'" (I replied) "And upon him be peace and may Allah bless him."[24]

Murshid Samuel Lewis had a saying, "The trouble with the church today is if you believe in angels, you're in; if you see them, you're out." In 'A'isha's time and place, a fifteen-year-old girl, intense and intuitive, might have actually experienced the angel. Did she yearn for some understanding of her husband's calling? Perhaps her ardor might blur the membrane between his powerful inner life and hers, and result in a moment on the threshold, a moment when Gabriel, bringer of the Words, became for 'A'isha her miracle as well as her husband's.

There were other surprises for 'A'isha. Muhammad introduced her to the arts. In her words: "…an Abyssinian woman [was] dancing with the boys around her. He [Muhammad] said. "Come and look, 'A'isha." So I went and placed my chin on the shoulder of Allah's Messenger and began to look at her over his shoulder."[25] Another time Muhammad, with 'A'isha in the Mosque, was resting with a cloth over his face while two young girls played the tambourine. Abu Bakr entered and scolded the girls for making noise. The Prophet uncovered his face and told him to let them play, because it was a kind of holiday and he saw no harm in it.

To read about 'A'isha is to be struck by her certainty, her deep trust in the mutual love between herself and Allah's Messenger. Certainty is everything in Islam.

flame, 'A'isha

She's certain, as she stands there laughing,
that the afternoon light arranges itself
around her beauty
    highlighting this, dappling that,
    throwing gold across her skin.
She's certain, and she'd tell you, that the man,

> Muhammad, lights her heart
> as she brightens his.
> > She believes in radiance
> > that lives in him
>
> and between them, a light that banishes the torment he calls
> *rust on the heart,*
> She's certain even their names are lit by this
> > sustaining flame,
> > present now and at the beginning of love.[26]

Here is the young woman, a teenager in those Medina years, in this line from a poem: "The tip ends of her loosened hair (are) like match fire in the back light…."[27] This invokes a back-lit girl with gold flecks in her eyes and a direct amused glance; leaning forward with enthusiasm. Each of those days, so full of life-changing movement, must have lasted a week. 'A'isha must have been continually melted down and reformed to withstand the force of her husband's accelerating evolution. Muhammad's inner circle would have been made up of followers in need, men and women who were envious, angry, aggrieved as well as filled with strength and optimism. 'A'isha held no option but to accept things as they were in her marriage. Given her age and her emotional landscape she demonstrated both courage and poise. From the constant irritant of jealousy, she endeavored to make a pearl.

Married young, the only life 'A'isha knew was Muhammad's life. Although she had no formal education, she had a fine mind and did not seem to care what others thought. She grew up in public with her husband's followers watching and often judging her critically. Both naïve and wise, she paid close attention to detail and missed nothing that went on around her. Her vigilance, combined with uneasiness about having to share her husband, made her a formidable foe. Before Asma's wedding, 'A'isha and another wife, Hafsa, helped the young bride get ready.[28] They hennaed her hands and combed her hair. They taught her to repeat a saying they claimed would make Muhammad love her more deeply. In fact, the saying was a formula for divorce. Once he heard it, the Prophet was forced to return her to her people. Through the wives' deception a potential rival disqualified herself before she went from bride to wife.[29]

"My wives are like the brothers of Joseph."

Was it her embroidered cloak
that made the Prophet's cunning women
whisper and scheme behind their veils?
Was it her lucent skin and satin hair

caused them to plot to have the stunning
Asma's innocence annul her?
Give her the words to say, they hissed,
when *ar-Rasul* first kneels to kiss her.

I take refuge in the Rahman from you.

And she, trusting the wives, could not
believe at first that, hidden in the loving oath
was her undoing, away *from you*, was
understood by everyone but her.

Sent home, un-husbanded, alone.
She left behind the embroidered cloak
as if bad luck was just another garment.

'A'isha wasn't always triumphant. Earlier, Muhammad, visiting a Companion, was attracted to his stunning wife, Zaynab. Muhammad took one look and fled. This incident led to her divorce from that close companion, Zayd. After Revelation confirmed that Muhammad was to marry Zaynab, and mentioned Muhammad sharing his time with his wives [Q. 33:51], 'A'isha commented tartly, "O, Allah's Apostle! I do not see but that your lord (Allah) hurries in pleasing you.[30]

Soon after Zaynab became his wife, Muhammad led an expedition to secure a well northwest of Mecca. There his soldiers scored a quick victory. Then he secured a tribe-to-tribe alliance by means of marriage to Juwayriyya, known to her people as Barra, the lovely daughter of the defeated chief. He met this young woman first when she appeared in the room he shared with 'A'isha, seeking help with her ransom:

'A'isha sees Juwayriyya

I had scarcely noticed her in the doorway of my room...
when I knew he would see in her what I saw.

— ('A'isha) Ibn Is-haq Sira[31]

She has the look of — by Allah! —
a woman to rescue,
this battle captive with *Rasul,*
and when they meet I'm here to see
her shimmer to feel her steal
my time with him.
She wets her lips, speaks legalese,
the syllables are running water;
gold bracelets on her arms move
like heat lightning. He offers
marriage and a name, *to save you*
from tragedy, he says. *Juwayriyya,* he says.

I've learned to sit through jealousy,
wrapped in tact while fire scorches
every tender part that claims him. He
sends her out, sees what I feel.
His eyes are kind. He asks,
Humaira, did you burn the meal?

'A'isha was beloved, but she was a high-tempered woman. Muhammad was lenient, but he never tolerated her jealousy toward his dead wife, Khadija. Once, when she spoke of Khadija in a moment of resentment as, "that toothless old woman who Allah replaced with a better," Muhammad replied, "Allah has not replaced her by a better. She believed in me when I was rejected; when they called me a liar, she proclaimed me truthful; when I was poor, she shared with me her wealth; and Allah granted me her children, though withholding those of other women."[32]

To her great sorrow, 'A'isha was unable to have a child. So much of a woman's identity within a peer group is about relationships with husband, parents, and children. Conversations and activities were centered on these three important groups. 'A'isha was left out of the gatherings of mothers and their little ones, although she was the right age for motherhood and most of the other wives were older. Birthing a child would distinguish her from the other wives, something she was denied.

wanting

'A'isha runs the names of newborns
through her milkless life.
She has a look as if she's found
an angel feather

with the promise of God's mercy
inscribed on it in gold.
She is holding the unborn
on the screen behind her eyes.

Now red runs down her legs
again. She bleeds and weeps.
The prophet's eyelashes are wet
as he carries a warm cup to her
like a mother.

'A'isha will not forget
the cramp at the center
of her love. She wants a child
more than anything. Consoling
Angels wait for a word from her,
an unpracticed gesture, even
a silence that implies
she longs for God this much.
Wings unfolded, they wait
to take the message home.

Then Mariya, the Christian Copt, arrived from Egypt and the Prophet became entranced with this foreigner whose status as a "wife" is disputed.
'A'isha reported that she had not been as jealous of any woman as she was of
Mariya. It was painful for her that Muhammad spent so much of his time
with another woman. Even after he moved her room to a place some distance from the mosque he continued to go there. This upset 'A'isha and the
others. Then Mariya became the only woman other than Khadija to carry
Muhammad's child. When she gave birth to Ibrahim, 'A'isha was despon-
dent. She knew she must be happy since Muhammad was overjoyed, but
she could not tolerate his enthusiasm, and let him know:

> Muhammad used to love carrying little Ibrahim around Medina. 'A'isha,
> however, refused to be impressed. 'Don't you think he is like me?' he would
> ask. 'I see no likeness', retorted 'A'isha. 'Look how plump he is and see his
> beautiful complexion!' enthused the Prophet. 'Anyone fed on sheep's milk is
> bound to be plump and fair,' 'A'isha replied tartly.[33]

It must have been his late-in-life fatherhood that Muhammad wanted to
share with his beloved wife. His happiness was not one she could share, nor

did it last. Ibrahim lived only two years. His father died six months after him.

Muhammad's complex family helped him maintain the balance between his inner life and his duties as a leader. He routinely slept only little each night, spending hours in prayer. Every day he was available to the *umma*. He visited his wives, milked his goats, fed his donkey, watered his camel, Qaswa, and played with the children. He was often taken with sweating and trembling when he received Revelation. He had excruciating headaches afterwards. His complete dedication to the Message took its physical toll.

'A'isha: Widow and Warrior

At the end of his life Muhammad became ill and was finally taken to 'A'isha's room. During his last hours, it was 'A'isha who held his head on her lap, eased his difficult and painful final passage.

privilege

My husband lay with his cheek on my lap
while death's small floating candles,
                    drifted close.

I kept watch on his breathing; held
to the thin rasp as if it were my own. Death
brightened him and trespassed
over our skin touch

and I said, "No!"

and he said, *There are as many ways
to Allah*... I could hardly hear Him
I said, "What?"
and he said,
        As many ways as there are mortal breaths.[34]

Around him danced a thousand glints of light.
I sensed the slow out-breath to death.
The room grew dark.
Then the lamb that was my heart
let out the first wail
as I fell into the fact — I was not dead.

> I despised, for many years, the privilege
> of being left alive.

After Muhammad's death 'A'isha's father, Abu Bakr, became the first *caliph*. 'A'isha, then eighteen, spent much of her time in service to the Prophet's Message and carried the title *Mother of Islam* for forty more years until her death. Scholars, leaders and the *umma* came to her for advice. She clarified traditions and interpreted jurisprudence; she was well respected for her excellent memory. She is credited with 2,210 hadith traditions, of which 1,210 are said to have been reported directly from Muhammad. One historian wisely comments, "While ('A'isha) may not have been above putting words in Mohammed's mouth when something she deemed important was at stake, the greater probability is that others, to suit their own purposes, put words in her mouth...."[35]

'A'isha's quarters were a kind of cemetery. This seems the strangest part of her story. Muhammad was buried there as well as Abu Bakr and 'Umar, the second *caliph*. She created a partition between her bed and the burial area, in a small room. The original burial site is today a marble rectangle more than fifty-three thousand feet square, but in those early years 'A'isha's everyday life went on in living quarters adjacent to the graves of her loved ones. The young widow offered the first two *caliphs* her support; they in turn honored her. But things were different under 'Uthman, the third *caliph*, who created a chaotic political environment by appointing family members and firing experienced people. When he punished a man unfairly, 'A'isha spoke out against him to a crowd: "She brought out a hair, a garment, and a sandal of the Prophet and, holding them for all to see, called out, "How quickly have you abandoned the *sunna* [practice] of your Prophet, when his hair, shirt, and his sandal have not yet decayed!"[36]

Political chaos escalated, with many of the *umma* wishing to have 'Uthman step down from his position; there was even some talk of murder. 'A'isha, disturbed by this extreme approach, distanced herself from the violence of Medina and chose instead to go on pilgrimage to Mecca. While she was away, 'Uthman was killed and 'Ali became the fourth *caliph*. 'Ali represented Muhammad's own family, the power center with its home in Medina, and was a change from the Quraysh tribal affiliation of the first three Meccan caliphs. He offered a general amnesty and supported a time of forgiveness and reconciliation. 'A'isha demanded that the killers be found and punished.

The Umayya, the clan connected to 'Uthman, encouraged 'A'isha as she pushed to hold 'Ali accountable for bringing the killers to justice. Remember, the Caliphate began with 'A'isha's father, which places her, by blood, on the side of the Meccans, or what came to be known as the *Sunnis.*

In the end, an army gathered around 'A'isha and rode against 'Ali, and a terrible bloodbath, called *The Battle of the Camel,* took place north of Basra in 656. This split was to fracture the followers of Islam for centuries.

'A'isha was forty-two that year. Her husband had been dead for twenty-four years; she had become an elder. She was always considered hot-headed, but just. The question of what moved 'A'isha to go to war at the head of an army is challenging. Her father had chosen not to support 'Ali as first caliph. It could have been her passion for fairness and the mandate of the Meccan ruling class, together with the grudge she held against 'Ali, from the time she was falsely accused of adultery. She mounted an enormous red camel and she rode with an army to Basra.

'A'isha either led, or was persuaded to lead, to use her power to right a perceived wrong. Some saw her as a passionate ring-leader. Others believe that she was being manipulated. In their view her action was a show of force, encouraged by the affiliates of the Quraysh, Mecca's old guard. Her aim as their representative would be reconciliation. A scholar from the succeeding era sounds a strong sympathetic note that 'A'isha as "Wife of the Prophet" believed she could prevail upon the fighting factions to negotiate for peace, that "they would be ashamed when she was present with them and stop fighting...[S]o she left her house to represent what Allah says: "If two parties among the Believers fall into a quarrel, make ye peace between them."[37]

She may have urged Hafsa and Umm Salama, to come with her, to join her cause. Hafsa said yes, but her brother forbade her to go. Umm Salama chided 'A'isha, reminded her to keep the "*jihad* of restraint," to stay secluded as Revelation said [Q. 33:33]. The followers of 'Ali made 'A'isha into an angry, villainous woman who misused her position as *Mother of the Faithful.* When one considers historical data on both sides, it becomes apparent that neither side wanted to negotiate. 'A'isha and her supporters wanted 'Ali to step down (since they felt he was morally responsible for 'Uthman's death), and called for an election to decide the calaphite. 'Ali, in turn, charged 'A'isha (and a prominent Meccan companion named Talha) of inciting the rebellion that led to 'Uthman's death.[38] This polarity marked the split between the *Sunni* ('A'isha and Talha, the Hashim, the Quraysh and some companions) and what came to be the *Shi'a* or the *Shi'atu 'Ali* (the Party of 'Ali.). This refers to those who supported first the Prophet's son-in-law, 'Ali, and after his death the grandchildren, Hasan and Husayn.

"Beware the barking dogs of Haw'ab" is a phrase from the legend of 'A'isha's journey to Basra.[39] In this tale, there were dogs in the town barking or howling. This caused 'A'isha to remember Muhammad's warning. Alarmed, she wished to turn back. But her generals, men invested in war, tricked her into going forward. Was this a story concocted by 'Ali's followers to discredit her? Whatever the truth, she continued, riding first to Basra, then to a place near the Tigris River where the armies faced each other and the leaders began to negotiate a resolution to the conflict. During the night fighting broke out and the truce ended quickly — with war.

owner's manual: the *howdah*

The father of this howdah is dawn with no birds. Its mother is a lost prayer. This is the story of 'A'isha, the ride to Basra, the sidewise motion of war. It is equal parts the camel's wobbly stride and a woman's keen eye.

The howdah is a covered platform strapped to a camel's back. Some facts about the howdah:

ONE.   It's arrowproof.
TWO.   One can peer out through the slits.
THREE.   Dismounting requires that the camel kneel or fall.

'A'isha travels inside a howdah.
When her army comes to *Haw'ab,* the local dogs
set up a ceaseless howl.
Beware the barking dogs of Haw'ab She hears him say,
"Turn back and do it now!" Were those the Prophet's words?

'A'isha's generals bark and bark around her. She wishes they'd shut up. She rides on.

❀❀ ❀❀

More things to know about the howdah:

ONE.   It's a fairly safe observation post in a battle
TWO.   Above the battle, it's a rallying point for the troops.
THREE.   It's a Pandora's Box.

❀❀ ❀❀

A war begins and ends in hemorrhage.
Ten thousand dead and dying men surround 'A'isha's tall, red camel.

❀❀ ❀❀

What happens to a howdah during a battle:

ONE.   In a fierce battle it can become a target.
TWO.   If the camel falls, the howdah crashes from a great height.
THREE.   *al Hawdaj, al Haddun!* The other side claims victory.

❀❀ ❀❀

The daughter of this story is a crushed bird. Its son is a desire for peace
folded into that unspeakable war. This is the story of 'A'isha
as *Shahada.* The story over and over, between one breath
and the next, anywhere else than this. Any other outcome.[40]

* *Shahada means witness (with a different vowel it is martyr)*

In the Battle of the Camel, 'A'isha lost everything except her life. 'Ali gave
her amnesty. He sent 'A'isha's brother, who was named Muhammad, to help
her out of the fallen howdah and pull an arrow from her upper arm. She
received an escort back to Medina where she faced her role in the deaths of
ten thousand Muslim men. Her failure to prevail caused a severe setback to
women's leadership. 'A'isha challenged the conservative status quo by riding
to battle for her beliefs. What if her side had been victorious? Better yet,
what if peace negotiations had succeeded under her leadership? Women's
governance may have been a possibility in the Muslim world. We will never
know. The door to the world of women's political participation slammed
shut with 'A'isha's defeat.[41]

Did the Qur'an discourage women leaders? The Qur'an does not forbid
women from exercising direct political rule; that is in the area of interpreta-

tion. The example often given is that the Queen of Sheba's right to rule is not questioned; the issue is her ignorance of monotheism [Q. 27:23].

The outrage of war — two great armies clashing on the battlefield — and the assault to 'A'isha's senses must have been brutal. This experience became a wound she carried for the remaining twenty-four years of her life.

'A'isha discovers how war can be

Because I was shocked by the sound
of a thousand laundrymen
beating cloth with paddles at the river —
or so it seemed,

I never heard, only saw
my guard fall,
his body flailing,
his mouth wide,
his feet digging in the ground;

never saw but sensed
the arrow pierce my arm
and stop at the bone, never took in
the camel scream, though
I felt the howdah tilt and crash.

Sometimes a dam breaks
and the whole town drowns.

I must help anyone not plan a war.[42]

'A'isha was consumed by terrible regret. "There are those who credit this childless widow of Muhammad with saying, 'It would be more to my liking had I remained in my house and not gone on my expedition to Basra than to have born ten noble and heroic sons to Muhammad.'"[43]

During the next quarter of a century 'A'isha kept the peace with 'Ali and remained in seclusion with her regrets. History agreed that she lived simply, wearing patched garments. She asked to be buried with the other wives in the Baqi' cemetery, not in her own apartment with her husband. "It is related when 'A'isha, peace be upon her, recited this verse, (Q. 33:33): "'Remain in your houses...' she was heard to weep until her head covering was wet."[44]

honeycomb: after the year 632

The day my husband died, the black
world, loud as a swarm of bees,
flew at me. I wrapped up
in death's white flag until the buzzing
ended and blue sky came back.
Rescued by words —
the ones he said to me and all I heard him say —
I turned and spoke them to his followers
my words, his words
like honey through the comb of me.
All thanks to God, I've been stung and blessed.

Ibn al-Abbas asked to see 'A'isha when she was dying. He praised her, and rejoiced that she would soon meet Muhammad. She said, "Leave me be, Ibn 'Abbas. By the one who has my soul in his hand, I wish that I had been something discarded and forgotten."[45] Her funeral was held at night and on the way to the Baqi' cemetery, multitudes of women, as if it were an *'id* celebration, turned out to honor her as her procession moved by the light of a palm branch that had been dipped in oil, ignited and burning. She died July 13, 678 at age sixty-four.

ZAYNAB, THE BEAUTIFUL

...We must risk delight. We can do without pleasure,
but not delight. Not enjoyment. We must have
the stubbornness to accept our gladness in the ruthless
furnace of the world.
...If the locomotive of the Lord runs us down,
we should give thanks that the end had magnitude.

Jack Gilbert, *A Brief for the Defense*

Zaynab b. Jahsh

AYNAB WAS KNOWN as "a beautiful woman" in nearly every recollection. She was family, the daughter of Muhammad's paternal aunt, and the wife of his adopted son Zayd. This marriage was based on Muhammad's wish rather than their feelings for each other.

One morning Zaynab opened the door to greet Muhammad and something happened between them. Some say she was wearing only a single garment, and that he closed his eyes and said, "Praised be God the Great, praised be God who turns hearts!"[46] They say he turned and he left quickly, not waiting for her husband, Zayd.

unwrapped (*al-kishaf*)

for Wendy TC

A veil was lifted, and her stillness
seized him there at the doorway, in a glare
of morning sun. Muhammad lost
his words, dropped composure into the well
of Zaynab's face, glance, and beauty mark;
then struggled to balance his voice on the spoon
of what he was about to say, so as not
to break the future like an egg.
And if the egg held something clear and
glorious — as in God's command, a wedding,
'Attar's hoopoe and the thirty birds passing
through seven valleys of love — then

then it's sure to happen: a tapping, cracks,
new life here in the open, unwrapped.[47]

Did he desire the wife of Zayd — the slave he received as a gift from Khadija, the man he had taught what he knew of the truth of Unity, the man he had freed and joined to his cousin Zaynab in marriage? These are explosive elements. Most historians agree that there was heat between the two, but some say that Allah's Messenger stepped in due to Revelation to make the best of a difficult divorce from a marriage he had instigated. He was the "honorable" friend. It was a practical choice for a failed marriage. This view saw them as a mismatched aristocrat with a one-time slave. She treated him badly and he wanted a divorce. "There is strong presumption that in the case of Zaynab b. Jahsh, Muhammad was not carried away by passion but was looking at the political implications of the match." At the same time, a Qur'anic commentator portrays "the strength of the attraction (between Muhammad and Zaynab) and its role in the marriage."[48] The strong version of what might have happened between Zaynab and Muhammad is forbidden love, the onset of impulsive feeling, deep connection, and pain.

It is not surprising that this struck Muhammad at a vulnerable time in 627 when the people known as "the hypocrites" were constantly eroding his political leadership. His old enemies, the Quraysh of Mecca, had forced him out of that city five years earlier, then killed many of the Companions at the battle of Uhud in 625. The Quraysh applied pressure to their business contacts in Medina. Muhammad was never certain which side these two-faced locals might take if Medina was challenged. He was married to four women, Sawda, 'A'isha, Hafsa, and Umm Salama. His resources were few. Hypocritical men played along with his teaching and lusted after his power and wives. Muhammad — father, teacher, husband, and bringer of Revelation from the One God — waited for guidance, with everyone watching.

In this charged atmosphere, Zaynab and Muhammad became the testing ground for a harmonious solution. She told her husband what was said and withdrew. Zayd addressed Muhammad three times, offering to step out of the marriage, deferring to his elder who told him to stay with his wife. Legally, there was a snag. Zayd was regarded as Muhammad's "son," and tribal law stated wisely that a man could not marry his son's wife. Zaynab's relatives were upset. With Zayd's divorce, she would have no choice but to return to them, even though she was near thirty years old. The community buzzed with opinions. The wives were unhappy. Muhammad was in the middle of a scandal.

The Prophet's attendant, Anas b. Malik was asked the most extraordinary thing he saw in the ten years he aided Muhammad, his answer was, "When the Messenger married Zaynab b. Jahsh."[49] The solution appeared with finality. The couple divorced. After some months direct Revelation commanded the Prophet to marry Zaynab — and pointed out she was married to an *adopted son*, not a blood son. The Prophet spoke God's words: [Q. 33:37]. "...when Zayd dissolves his marriage with her (Zaynab), we join her in marriage to you." Order was restored in the community. When she was informed of this she gave silver ornaments (some say coins or jewelry) to the one who brought the message, then prostrated and agreed to fast for two months for Allah. It appears that she internalized her deep moment of joy and relief.

Muhammad invited the entire community and people off the street to the wedding supper. It was said that the Messenger of Allah did not have a wedding feast for any of his wives as he had for her. He sacrificed a sheep. Another source explains dramatically that food was scarce. The small amount of date-paste grew until seventy-two people ate their fill. It was a "loaves and fishes" situation, coming at a time of impoverishment in Muhammad's community, a real celebration. But how was the wedding feast for her? No other women are mentioned, except a reference to the wives in their own dwellings. It must have been an awkward time, becoming more so as the evening wore on.

Zaynab's wedding meal: a sonnet

for Taj

End the meal. We're done. The groom says and he stands,
then goes to underscore his words. She yawns.
The bride is on display; the Prophet's wife, and
she's more stunning than they'd heard, a headstrong
girl. She gazes at a drowning silver moth
inside her cup, at flies on mutton bones,
a stain on an embroidered wedding cloth.
Oh, how she'd like to make this night her own.
But men are here, and stay and yak and eye
the girl by lamplight. Then smoke relieves her.
They rub their eyes and swear, but don't reply
when asked why wicks flame clean after they leave her.

The vulgar never comprehend good manners.
A little burn — *adab* inscribed on banners.

adab. Important principle in the Muslim world; polite, refined behavior.

What followed has been greatly misunderstood. The subject of the veil can be traced to this very long evening. The newly married couple had been hosting the public for hours. People on the street had been invited and fed. The pressure on the bride was considerable. We know she was lovely. She must have suffered under the crude looks of curiosity and lust, and had no shelter from this. When the guests finally left, Muhammad went to lower a curtain, a room divider, at the same time he was saying goodnight to his servant, Anas. New words of Revelation were spoken aloud as the curtain fell, separating the two men. The Words of God were not meant as a segregation law for women, but instead a message meant for those inside the *umma;* an assurance that privacy was to be a part of their previously public lives [Q. 33:53].

> O ye who believe! Enter not the dwellings of the Prophet for a meal without waiting for the proper time, unless permission is given. But if you're invited then enter, and when your meal is ended then disperse. Linger not for conversation. Lo! That would cause annoyance to the Prophet, and he would be shy of [asking] you [to go]; But Allah is not shy of the truth. And when ye ask of them [the wives of the Prophet] anything, ask it of them from behind a curtain (*hijab*). That is purer for your hearts and their hearts.

The word *hijab* means to both separate and protect. This verse is about etiquette and the lack of it, about behavior when entering a house. The intention, it is clear, was not about protecting women from change and shutting them in their rooms. That came with the patriarchal interpretation that arrived in the decades, then centuries following the death of Allah's Messenger (*Rasul*). At the time of this verse, strangers appeared daily in the part of Medina where Muhammad lived, in the mosque, and even in the rooms belonging to his wives, to seek audience with Allah's Messenger. This was especially true in 627 after the Battle of the Trench, when the Message of the Prophet became a magnet for those impressed by his stunning victory. 'Umar spoke to Muhammad on several occasions about protecting his wives. Men increasingly harassed the women companions as they went about their business — and they did, since everyone was free to participate in communal activities. It was not long before the next verse addressed female modesty [Q. 24:31].

> "And tell the believing women to lower their gaze and be mindful of their chastity, and not to display their charms [in public] beyond what may [decently] be apparent thereof. Hence, let them draw their head coverings over their bosoms and not display [more of] their charms [adornment] to any but their husbands...." (This continues with a list of males with whom they can feel at home — fathers, fathers-in-law, sons, brothers, young boys, nephews, attendants, etc.)

And more directly [Q. 33:59]: "O Prophet! Tell your wives and daughters and the believing women to draw their outer garments closely round themselves. That makes it more likely that they will be recognized and not be harmed." A commentator, al-Hasan, explains that at this time women of the *umma* experienced a serious problem — town men were bothering them: A free woman (not a slave, concubine) used to go out and be thought a slave girl and be pestered. So Revelation told the women of the household to draw their outer garments closely around themselves.

These *suras* were concerned with safeguarding women outside their homes. The Prophet's wives were the examples to the communities in Medina and everywhere that Islam was spreading. It was, however, much later when Islam expanded into what were previously the Byzantine and Persian Empires that the practice of veiling and seclusion for nobility worked its way into the law for all women.

Zaynab's legacy suggests to me two attributes of Allah, the Hidden and the Revealed: *al-batin* and *az-zahir*. On the one hand, these esoteric Names refer to work on one's inner state and ripening of personal magnetism. On the other, this pair might incorporate a gesture or its implication; for example the power or beauty of that which is concealed in plain sight, or held back, especially in a social matrix around a prophet, where visibility may be carefully considered. The intensity — a kind of hide and seek, where one is inside the other and one reveals the other — is the essence of the next poem.

swaying lamps

The beautiful Zaynab holds a moon splinter for a mirror.

> She presses a kohl twig to each lower lid
> and sweeps it
> across inside the lashes,
> smudges with a blackened fingertip;
> then begins to pray.

Kohl and prayer together.
A dark tree lit by swaying lamps.

On melancholy evenings
her light is fierce.

When the man she loves looks in
her eyes, he sees a crash of light

hears the spool of her breath unwind.

Muhammad yearns to touch her with perfume,
have a private moment with her, a screen
to honor their time alone, a curtain
in the room so he can loosen it.

Let cloth cascade!

Released in air between earth and stars —
fabric that covers so many women
identifies them, connects them,

sets them apart

began this way — as a simple gesture of modesty.

The intimacy of Zaynab's story leads us deeper: It may be the nature of life
in the everyday world to feel a separating membrane between one's inner-
most questions and the vastness of God. Al-'Alawi, a Sufi master, once said:
"It is not a question of knowing God when the veil is lifted but of knowing
God in the veil itself."[50]

Concentrate on Zaynab's character and she begins to vanish, pulled into a
private, interior world of frequent remembrance of Allah and Spartan needs.
Umm Salama calls her "a righteous woman who fasted and prayed, and
worked and gave all (she earned) as charity to the poor."[51] When 'A'isha was
wrongly accused of adultery, Zaynab defended her to Muhammad. 'A'isha
repaid that loyalty when Zaynab was sent by the other wives to ask Muhammad to be more impartial with the hours that he gave generously to 'A'isha.
Fatima, Muhammad's daughter, had returned earlier without success. The
women persisted. Much later, 'A'isha recalled the day in this hadith:

> The wives of Allah's Apostle then sent Zaynab b. Jahsh, also the wife of Al-
> lah's Apostle, who was somewhat equal in rank with me in [his] eyes.
> I have never seen a woman more advanced in religious devotion than Zay-
> nab, more God-conscious, more truthful, more alive to the ties of blood,
> more generous and self-sacrificing in practical life and having more chari-
> table disposition and thus nearer to Allah, the Exalted, than her. Allah's
> Messenger permitted her to enter ... She lost her temper quickly but was
> soon calm. She said: "Allah's Messenger, your wives have sent me to you

seeking equity in case of ['A'isha]." She then came to me and showed harshness, and I was watching the eyes of Allah's Messenger [to see] whether he would permit me. Zaynab went on until I came to know that [he] would not disapprove if I retorted. Then I exchanged hot words until she was reduced to silence. Then Allah's Messenger smiled…[52]

'A'isha honored her rival for her strengths, then used her famous wit to win the debate. The mixture of generosity and what 'A'isha calls "religious devotion," inspired Zaynab's love of service. The "People of the Bench, the Intimate Friends of Allah" sat on a plank near the simple mosque and chanted the Names of God.[53] Most were homeless and supported by the community. Imagine Zaynab, absorbed in what may be called mysticism:

Zaynab and the people of the bench

for Art

God Lovers
magnify each crack
of light in night's monotony,
arouse the dawn,
intone: *Allah, Allah* from the wooden bench.

God Lovers
graze camels on *la ilaha illa 'llah,*
water vast herds with life-giving sound,
drizzle it across
an afternoon sun nothing is new under.

The grit and zeal of God Lovers
bring Zaynab to tears. She
feeds them her own modest supper.
Dhikr and the desert air at nightfall
oversee and instruct the darkness.

God Lovers
don't stop for anything. *The angels
hold hands with them night and day;*
so said Muhammad, and someone
wrote it down.

It's been mentioned the family ties were very close. Zaynab would say to her husband-cousin Muhammad, "I am the daughter of your paternal aunt, and you have no kin among your wives but me." [54] She suffered from pride and the tendency to hold her connections over the wives: "She used to boast to the other wives of the Prophet, saying, 'I am the most honored among you because of the One (Allah) who gave me in marriage and the one (Gabriel) who was my intermediary.'"[55] Another hadith brings to light her mixture of anti-Semitism and jealousy. Muhammad asked her to lend Safiyya a camel, but she spoke an ethnic slur and denied the Jewish wife the use of an extra animal. It is written that Muhammad became so angry he left her alone for three months. Some local Jews had not been friendly. Safiyya's kin were the newly defeated enemy from a nearby city. Zaynab was not the only one suffering from a proud xenophobia, shown in this kinship mode expressed by the Bedouin proverb: "My brothers and I against my cousin, my cousin and I against the stranger."

She often put others before her, perhaps as an antidote to her flaws. Zaynab excelled in handwork. According to 'A'isha, she tanned and pierced leather, and embellished cloth with embroidery; sold what she made; bought food, then took the food she cooked and gave it the hungry. She was so generous that there is a famous hadith spoken by Prophet Muhammad: "The swiftest of you to join me (in paradise) will be the one with the longest armspan (or hand)." The wives measured each other's reach. Zaynab was a small woman, yet when she died, it was clear that Muhammad had been talking about generosity. "We came to know that the long hand was a symbol of practicing charity, so she was the first to follow the Prophet." [56] The poor, who relied on her were grief-stricken that death had taken their angel of charity.

Zaynab would have seen her fellow wives as individuals who cared for the welfare of Muhammad as well as for each other and the greater *umma*. The small internal squabbles and alliances became unimportant when seen through this unifying lens. There was diversity; Rayhana and Safiyya were Jews, not Arabs; while Mariya (perhaps a "wife," perhaps not) was an Egyptian Copt. There were age differences; Sawda was old enough to be the mother of several of the young women, while Hafsa and 'A'isha were spirited youth one minute and serious, perceptive adults the next. Juwayriyya was from a neighboring tribe that the *umma* defeated. Umm Habiba was the daughter of the Meccan enemy chief. Maymuna lived in Mecca also.

'A'isha, a favorite, mentions that Zaynab and Umm Salama gave council to Muhammad and helped with decisions. The following hadith story of a childish prank demonstrates how closely the youngest wives watched Allah's Messenger. In the poem, Revelation plays the umpire when Muhammad promises to deny his own pleasure for the sake of family harmony.

Zaynab and the honey

He utters *oh*, with his
eyes closed, then starts to laugh.
She sits across from him and pours.
The cup is small.
Whoever heard of drinking honey straight?

The door ajar, a blur of skirts and whispers.
the taller one pulls the other girl away.
"Forget them. Just say —
Husband, your breath stinks of manna gum.
I'll say it too."

One rolls her eyes, the other holds her nose.
He strokes his beard and his beard is sticky. *Oh.*
He tells them: *I have drunk honey*
with Zaynab b. Jahsh. I won't do it again.[57]
But didn't Revelation say:
Why do you make forbidden
what Allah has made lawful for you?

He heads back to Zaynab's.

The word *delicious* sounds better spoken loudly.
She asks if he'd like to sip from her cupped hands.
Her wide smile. The perfect, straight white teeth.
Messenger of Allah, may this sweeten our days and nights.

oh.

When 'Umar sent money to each of the wives as a pension after the Prophet died, Zaynab shielded herself from the sight of it. In 642, ten years after Muhammad's death, Zaynab was the first wife to die. She left instructions about the piece of cloth used to lower her into the grave — "If you can, give away my waist-wrapper as charity (*sadaqa*) when you lower me down" —

making sure every single physical object that had been hers was offered to the poor.[58] An Abyssinian style bier, with a cloth over her body, was used to carry her to the grave. 'Umar, then the *caliph*, spoke the prayers over her body. The disenfranchised were bereft. She had taken care of so many, now she was gone, leaving nothing but the fragrance of a generous life well lived.

UMM SALAMA, MOTHER OF PEACE

O lucky humankind! If the love
which guides the heavens guides your souls.

Boethius, *Love is Lord of All*
Quote trans. Paula Saffire

Umm Salama, mother of peace

Once I was a child who galloped bareback
on the forbidden stallion. No bridle.
Flat against his neck, eyes open, flying.

A GIRL CALLED HIND, who later became Umm Salama, was born
into an aristocratic family famous for its horsemen. Her father
was Abi Umayya b. Mughira, a Qurayshi noble of the prominent
Makhzum clan, leaders of Muhammad's opposition in Mecca.[59]

In her teens, Hind, a matriarchal youth, chose 'Abdullah b. al-Asad as
her husband. 'Abdullah was a Makhzum cousin of her two half-brothers,
and the privileged couple was expected to follow tradition—respecting the
family gods, becoming part of Mecca's power structure. But the Prophet's
words appealed to the young couple. Their parents, who had been delighted
when the couple married, were equally dismayed when it was discovered
they had joined Muhammad's disreputable group.

Abyssinia

When violence exploded against his followers in Mecca, the Prophet sought
a place to send them out of harm's way. He chose Abyssinia where, years
before, his great grandfather, Hashim and his brothers made treaties that allowed them to engage in business there.[60] Seventh-century Ethiopia, Sudan,
and parts of southern Egypt shone under a benevolent Christian king called
the *najashi* (Ar) or *negus* (Ge'ez), whose authority may have stretched back
into the ancient world to Bilqis, the Queen of Sheba.[61] This ruler supported
the Arabian Prophet and opened his capital city, Aksum, to Muhammad's
followers. Abyssinia was a grueling week's journey from Mecca by camel,
ship, and mule, but up to one hundred of the Prophet's faithful departed
from the old Red Sea port of Shu'ayba, and sailed south to the Abyssinian
port of Adulis. Among the first to leave in 615 were Hind (Umm Salama)
and her husband, who traveled with the Prophet's daughter Ruqayya and
her husband, 'Uthman. Later, they would be joined by Ramla (Umm Habiba) and her husband.[62] It was an optional custom for Arabic woman to take
the *kunyas* (honorific titles: *Umm* — mother of...) and the names of their
first children, Salama and Habiba.[63]

The move away from Arabia would have created a challenge for even the bravest of the exiles. They would need to arrange travel. [64] Perhaps 'Uthman b. Affan or some other wealthy Companion could pay for the trip or the *Nejashi* might have sent a boat for them. The Red Sea runs deep and is surprisingly wide, 300 miles or more — adding some longitudinal distance between ports. The Ethiopian headlands of Abyssinia in those days were forest — unlike much of Arabia, especially the bare, nearly dry eastern shore, known as the Hijaz. The first boat of ten travelers may have felt the heat of a summer crossing, pushed through days and cooler nights by prevailing northwest winds. Occasional sand storms would have created a terrifying brown tempest that foiled navigation.

land

When we reached Abyssinia, the Negus received us with kindness.[65]

for Hamza El-Din

It is by God's Grace
that a small boat —
that sloshing water camel —
blown west
across a salt sea,   a following sea

a sea lit by *the night traveler*
and other stars,
reached the far shore.

It is by the Grace of God
a woman's ebony hand
offers a dry towel,
and this cool water in a cup
provokes my tears
a disarray of humped up sobs.

It is by God's Grace
I, Hind, am here; a sailed-in
fact. It is nothing like
I thought, run aground,
split wide by kindness
laughing and crying,
feet on the soil.

To sedentary Meccans, this was another world entirely: flora, language, and skin color. The smell of the land, the look of the animals and the offered food surprised them. The journey to Aksum by mule took the refugees through the hilly area between the coast and the upland, which in that era may have been thick with forests. The uphill distance from the coast insured the city's continued existence in a time when the Abyssinian Empire was waning.

Hind in Africa: leaving the Red Sea

Riding inland,
her pony,
her pack mules,
her thoughts
push through wet leaves.
She has no words for what she sees
or hears. Her camels
left behind days ago —
what is a rhinoceros to her?

In rain as warm as salt broth,
the jungle gasp,
the sloshing mud,
the orchids to duck under,
a woman's mind can waver
reason shift;
She tries humming,
breathes sacred phrases,
imagines herself calm.
Nothing works.

But, in the fruit-bat dark,
brushed by
looping snake vines,
she recognizes some
wild grace, the wind's fingers,
their blessing
like a distant mother's touch
those full-moon hands
on her hair.

Ethiopian legend places the Ark of the Covenant in Aksum, which was also a center of devotion to Mary, the Mother of Jesus. The city is the home of the Queen of Sheba's ruined palace, where the pools are still in use. It is a place with mysterious obelisks, ancient grave markers of royalty. Aksum traded in rhinoceros horn and hippopotamus hide; emeralds, ivory and obsidian; tortoise shell and salt. Its gold and silver coins, bearing the name and image of the Negus, were used to trade with Rome, Byzantium, Persia, and Egypt. Aswan was 30 days north, the headwaters of the Blue Nile, nearby.

What did Umm Salama learn? Hear? Witness? What happened to the hadith describing her own experience? What stories did they carry home to the community? Hadith leaves us with less than recipes and cloth, implements and funeral customs, mentions a medicine that Muhammad disdained. But here an ancient and venerable civilization, so removed from these desert people welcomed them and gave them refuge.

The Companions came, recited Qur'an, and stayed for several years and more. Some settled there until Mecca was reclaimed in 630, others permanently. The Muslim community in Aksum is older than that of Medina. In those days, what became known as "Islam" was fluid. Without the name "Muslim," its followers were known as the *umma*. By then, Christianity had been alive for over six hundred years and in Aksum for more than two hundred. In contrast, the newcomers had a contemporary vision of the Biblical message. The Qur'an contains pages of stories about the Old Testament prophets. Mecca's children had allegiance to Allah's Messenger. They had their prayers. They had a few years of Revelation's teaching, mostly concerned with the goodness and power of God, encouraging gratitude, worship, generosity, and purification. They were given warnings about consequences of selfish and greedy behavior. Less than half the Qur'an had been revealed. Muhammad had just begun to speak against idol worship and for One God.

For centuries after the Prophet's death, Christian Abyssinia and Egypt were respected by the conquering Muslim soldiers. There was the image of Mary and infant Jesus in the Ka'ba that Muhammad protected when the idols were broken.[66] Perhaps the later literalists tore the Old and New Testament from the work Muhammad was doing when it served their purposes. Xenophobia was the likely knife that cut all connecting lines between a single God and a single message to the children of Abraham from the prophets. What was Muhammad's larger plan? What went on here in Abyssinia around the year 615 seems buried by later prejudice. The Muslims who lived after this era mention that this was the first "Muslim" settlement outside Arabia. They tell the story of the Mary Sura mentioned here. But little else is remembered of this rich sister culture across the Red Sea, the people who reached out to the persecuted Arabs and offered them a home.

It was in the court of the king that a recitation of the *Sura of Mary* took place [Q. 19:1–36] as a test of these mostly young people. Fortunately, Umm Salama's words were preserved as a record in hadith. We learn the details of this historic moment because her credibility was strong enough to endure. She related that two envoys of the Meccan enemy arrived in Aksum soon after the immigrants. They offered the Negus a bribe to return their children, and argued that the young people had been led astray by a fanatic named Muhammad. The king, a thoughtful man, sent for the Arab immigrants and for his bishops, who were known for recognizing sincere devotion. He asked the Companions of the Prophet to give him a good reason not to take mule loads of hides in exchange for their return. Ja'far b. Abi Talib spoke:

> ...God sent us a Messenger from out of our midst, one whose lineage we knew, and his veracity and his worthiness of trust and his integrity. He called us unto Allah, that we should testify to His Oneness and worship Him and renounce what we and our fathers had worshiped in the way of stones and idols; and he commanded us to speak truly, to fulfill our promise. [W]e have been happy in your protection, and it is our hope, O King, that here, with you, we shall not suffer wrong.[67]

The Negus asked if they had any Revelation of their Prophet. Ja'far recited a passage from the *Sura of Mary*, revealed just before they left for Aksum [Q. 19:16–21]. The following is this New Testament story contained in the Qur'an:

> Commemorate Mary in the Book, when she withdrew from her people unto a place in the East, and took cover from them, We sent a spirit of Ours to her who appeared before her in the concrete form of a man. "I seek refuge in the Merciful from you, if you fear Him," she said. He replied, "I am only a messenger from thy Lord, sent to bestow a good son on you." "How can I have a son," she said, "when no man hath touched me, nor am I sinful?" "Thus will it be. Your Lord said: 'It is easy for Me,' and that:' We shall make him a sign for men and a blessing from Us.'"

(Ahmed 'Ali, translation)

Umm Salama tells that the Negus and the bishops wept as Ja'far recited, and again when they heard the translation. Then he told the envoys to go back to Mecca, and the young Companions that they were welcome to stay.

The next day, the envoys went again to the Negus and said Muhammad's Companions had lied; that they really believed Jesus was a "slave." Again the emperor sent for the exiled people and asked them to explain. Ja'far replied, "We say of him what our Prophet brought to us, that he is the slave of God and His Messenger and His Spirit and His Word which he cast unto Mary the Blessed Virgin." The Negus then replied to Ja'far and the others, "You are safe in my land. Not for mountains of gold would I harm a single one of you!"[68] In that moment Muhammad's new faith and Christianity joined in respect. Perhaps Umm Salama and the others felt their connection to Christianity through their shared story of Mary's annunciation. Perhaps, in that great center of Mary's worship, she could feel at home.

In the city center the obelisks of Aksum still stand, impermeable, mysterious. Although some lie fallen, they are no less compelling today than they were in the time of the Negus. They probably amazed Hind, unaccustomed to such splendid monuments, or anything sculptural commemorating the dead.

Hind's vision

Near dawn,
I crossed
the field
of obelisks,
granite shafts
tall and silent,
story stacked
on story
on every one,
carved doors
and windows,
pretend to let
me in. There
is no entry
just the carving
of a knocker.
I reach
to touch it,
I get so close

my feet rock
on the sill,
that marks
a door as if
there were a door,
as if the green
bird singing
on the tower
sang the words
O Peacemaker.

The new land wasn't easy for desert dwellers. The terrain was mountainous; for months rough winter reigned.[69] The cold, damp Companions shivered and longed for their families and their teacher, Muhammad. There were some deaths, one family erased by poisoned water. Ramla, daughter of the Meccan leader Abu Sufyan, like Hind, came from a noble family of Mecca. Her daughter, Habiba was born in exile and Ramla became Umm Habiba. She spent years in Aksum, and remained loyal to Muhammad and the *umma* even after her husband converted to Christianity. Later she became Muhammad's wife.

Mecca and Medina

Hind too, gave birth to a boy named Salama (which means "peace" and gave her the *kunya*, Umm Salama, "mother of peace"). Hind's husband, 'Abdullah, became Abu Salama (Abu meaning "father of" the child Salama). Umm Salama and her family were among the first to leave for Mecca but instead of a homecoming, the exiles were exposed to more harsh treatment. The antagonism between the Meccans and the *umma* was worse than before. The Messenger's protecting uncle and Khadija had died the same year. Muhammad received an invitation to move north to Medina (known as Yathrib), to mediate between rival factions. It was decided that a few followers would go ahead to prepare for the community to move north. Abu Salama took his wife and son and rode out of Mecca one morning. Before he reached the edge of town he was stopped by men from Umm Salama's clan, who took the camel with Umm Salama and the child. Abu Salama was unable to free his family and so rode north to Medina alone. On the way to Umm Salama's father's house, a group from Abu Salama's tribe appeared and the grandmothers fought over the child, dislocating his shoulder. From a poem fragment:

> Surrender I learned from *Rasulullah,* and
> from the time Salama's grandmothers tugged
> his bones apart. The men held me back.
> I spat in the road to let the old ones know;
> I saw you. Inside my powerlessness — Ya Aziz!

Umm Salama was confined to her parents' house and little Salama went with the paternal grandparents. From her parent's point of view, she was in a dangerous cult and needed to be brought to her senses. Confined there for nearly a year away from husband and child, we can only imagine her sorrow, the strength of her resolve, the depth of her prayers.

That year, an attempt was made on Muhammad's life, but he escaped from Mecca, was followed by trackers, and hid in a cave in the desert with Abu Bakr. A spider wove a web across the opening, and a bird made a hasty nest — hiding them miraculously. When danger passed, the two traveled safely to Medina and set up a new life there with the *umma* for the next ten years. Many Meccans followed him there. This was known as the *hijra* or migration. The Muslim calendar then began with the year 622.

When Umm Salama's family released her, the in-laws gave her the child and a camel, but no escort. Determined, she headed out of town alone, pointing her camel north. The keeper of the keys to the Ka'ba, 'Uthman b. Talhah asked her where she was going and who was with her. She told him Allah was her escort. 'Uthman took the camel's lead rope and walked with her three days and nights to the outskirts of Medina, where she was met by overjoyed friends and reunited with her husband. She had only glowing praise for the honorable 'Uthman, not yet a Muslim. In the next few years, Umm Salama had three more children. When her husband was dying from a battle wound, Muhammad promised him to take care of his wife. Abu Salama soon died and the Prophet proposed marriage, but Umm Salama declined, saying she was prone to jealousy, had four children, and was too old (almost thirty). Muhammad persuaded her and they were married. Her close friends in the *umma* were Fatima and 'Ali. Other allies among the wives were Umm Habiba and Sawda, who shared her exile in Abyssinia. All of them but Sawda were parents raising children.

As wife of Muhammad, Umm Salama was a leader. She was intelligent, well spoken, and unafraid to stand for what she believed. She handed down 378 hadith. Once she confronted 'Umar, demanding he stop meddling in the business of Muhammad's women. She did more than that. Scholar Linda Kern translates the confrontation: "...[Umar] remarks (later) that Umm Salama really "shook him up" or, literally "seized him a seizing." She "broke" him, *kasara*, from something of what he was "experiencing as a painful state of agitation" *kunta ajidu*... Her remarks pierced his "agitated state," and calmed him down a bit."[70] This passage of hadith reveals her strength and ability to work with difficult people. Umm Salama was self-disciplined. She fasted every Monday, Thursday, and Friday, and kept the midnight optional prayers, making her inner life strong. She was a bright and dependable woman in Muhammad's life.

After the *hijra*, Meccan leaders put together a small army to ride against Muhammad. Now his nonviolent position changed. Revelation commanded the *umma* to stand up to the Meccan soldiers. The era of war had begun [Q. 22:39–40].[71] Muhammad took Umm Salama to Hudaybiya, the Battle of the Trench, and the Overthrow of Mecca. Not all his wives had the stomach for this kind of activity. She wasn't a participant, although she kept his tent for him near the battle zone. An early success known as "the Battle of the Trench," in 627, came from the suggestion of a Persian, an ex-slave who followed Muhammad. Using a trench to break an opposing army's charge was an idea unknown in Arabia before Medina was defended in this way. During battle, a vastly superior Meccan army had no strategy to deal with such a barrier and was defeated by a combination of this new technology and by a storm that came in at night and blew their tents away. During the clash, Umm Salama stayed in a tent set up for the Prophet near the battle. She took care of her husband while the sounds of swords and axes rattled her bones. Mistress of a harsh desert code, she didn't swerve but cooked and prayed and carried water until Medina triumphed.

Referred to by the women as "Umm Salama the Wise," she was highly regarded. The most famous story of her wisdom is the Treaty of Hudaybiya, a crucial moment in Muhammad's life when he enacted a peace treaty with the leaders of Mecca. The trials upset his followers, who felt that Muhammad had given away too much in negotiation. He was then moved to bring the group to a deeper commitment. Each man made a pledge. But the feeling of that unified moment of trust was soon over. They were tested more severely by the Meccans and protested when Muhammad signed a peace accord, which seemed to offer the pilgrims almost nothing, stating that they would abort their pilgrimage to Mecca that year. He then asked them to perform the ritual sacrifice as if they were in the *hajj*. His clear directive to the fourteen hundred people was coldly ignored. In this crisis he went to Umm Salama and asked for advice. She said: "Prophet of God, do you approve of this? Go out and speak not a word to any of them until you have slaughtered your fattened camel and summoned your shaver to shave your hair."[72] When the people saw Muhammad complete the actions he had told them to do, the stunned mood was broken.

Umm Salama at Hudaybiya

i.
They come on foot, camelback
and mule; they don't know
what they came for as they crouch
in the sand. A pilgrimage to nowhere,
those sullen men, hollow with doubt.

ii.
They speak a vow
next to the yellow tree,
each of a thousand men *take hand*
with God's Messenger, each man
offers the *ridwan* pledge.
I see it all.

iii.
The cooking smoke changes direction,
shifts back, carries words that burn
my eyes. He's heard the talk,
"leader astray," asks me
what to do. I mention ritual
head shaving, a sharp blade
that polishes the scalp as the hair falls,
or animal offering, a sharp blade
a blood-burst in the throat of the ram,
our old way of joining. Tribal men
know this erases doubt so each man speaks
directly to Allah, remembering why he's here.

Revelation confirmed the Messenger's strategy with the chapter of *Victory
(al-fath)* [Q. 48:1–29]. "Allah sent down *sakina* (tranquil Presence) into
the hearts of "those who stay true to a trust" (a translation more true to the
Arabic than 'believers') the *mumin,* that they may add faith to their faith…"
[Q. 48:4]. It can then be said that Umm Salama guided a key moment in
the negotiations and support of a crucial peace treaty. It was the beginning
of a revolutionary approach to disputes. A historian reports, "No previous
victory in Islam was greater than this. There was nothing but battle when
men met; but when there was armistice and war was abolished and men
met in safety and consulted together, none talked about Islam intelligently
without entering it."[73]

Umm Salama's position at Muhammad's side reached a high point on
the day he entered Mecca to claim the city in the name of Islam. Umm
Salama, Maymuna, (last wife of the Prophet) as well as Fatima and 'Ali were
along. This promised return was bittersweet, since Mecca had broken the
Hudaybiya treaty with the *umma*. Muhammad marched on the city with a
large army. He took it without bloodshed. The first thing he did after de-
claring a general amnesty was to break the idols in the Ka'ba.

Umm Salama tells of breaking the idols

for Shabda

To speak of the day of breaking
to you who never broke
open or fell awake with a thud and shattering is vanity.

Not just the people of Islam, all Mecca watched.

What was broken broke for *wholeness.*
Three hundred sixty gods dragged from the Ka'ba;
their weight tore the skin of the ground.

In the center, The Prophet
slow walked his camel around the shrine, stopped
before each statue to point his staff
at what kept us apart. We heard him say:

Reality is now. The unreal vanishes! The unreal vanishes![74]

Terracotta lurched and dropped off its pedestal.
Stone fell. Cracks ran through us all.
I stood by Muhammad's leather tent.
His back was dark with sweat.

That night, when Allah's Work was only shards and dust,
I lay beside my husband in the dark
and knew that this day — like the earlobe of a new-born
child, like water lifted from the well —

returned us to ourselves.

After accepting Mecca's surrender, Muhammad declared a general amnesty
to everyone, including most of his enemies. Although tribal law now made
the Meccans his property, Muhammad declared all men, women, and slaves
to be free, and the people took an oath of allegiance to never wage war on
Muhammad. Remarkably, no one was forced to convert to Islam.

After the triumph of Mecca, Islam became the bright star of the Arabian peninsula and eclipsed the whole Middle East and beyond — Persia,
Rome, and Abyssinia. It was a joyful and exciting time. Allah's Messenger's
work was nearly done. Within two years, Muhammad fell ill and soon died.
Umm Salama articulates shock and despair:

Umm Salama's mourning ghazal

for Robert Bly

I keep Muhammad's beard hair in this locket now.
You can't tell how he looked; the way he grinned at me,
the toothstick rubbing those white teeth, cat in his lap.

I put his sheepskin to my face to hold him close —
by smell. Some say, O, *Mother of the Faithful,*
look after us! But I remind them, I'm cry-blinded.

I am a burning palm; heart and greenery on fire.
A white she-camel sobs and bellows at the well
as the night sky sends in angel firefighters.

The Prophet is a golden bird; feathers tethered
to Allah, lit like Gabriel. I remember the ostrich.
We watched it run; he joked with bird puns.

My husband's black turban furls a field of peace.
I know the cloth by heart. Each spiral turn and twist;
an unembellished dome, the word *salam*, inside.

Until she passed away, Umm Salama lived as a "Mother of Islam," a secluded lamp of hope, teaching her family and those who came for guidance,
watching what her husband's work had become, but most of all, following
the stories of her children and Fatima and 'Ali. She was consulted by scholars and valued for her interpretation of legal issues.[75] She was about thirty-
seven when she became a widow. She died at age eight-six, which is very,
very old, by the standards of the day. If most women became mothers before
age sixteen, she was many times over a great-grandparent.

In her last days, terrible things were happening to Islam. Muhammad
appeared to her in a dream, very upset and told her that his last grandson,
Husayn has just been murdered. It was true. This disaster in a place called
Karbala made a great wound in the body of Islam that has never healed.
Umm Salama died soon after.

calamity

"The Prophet unwraps his turban and throws dirt on his head."[76]

She's shaken, waking from this.
It's just a dream, for God's sake.
Husband, Allah's Messenger,
dead for fifty years, and all,
her mattress screaming: *al-qari'a — calamity!*
She knows that verse:

What can tell you of the qari'a?
A day people are like scattered moths,
and mountains — fluffed carded wool.[77]

She makes ablution, *salat*, and says to herself:

daylight now, the mountains look fine
and people around here,
most of them lack the sense of moths,
don't know fire and light from darkness.

There should be messengers from Persia coming,
with five days of hard riding

unless I dreamed the whole thing up.
She tells her mattress to shut up,
invokes the Protector
but *al-qari'a's* alarm goes on.
Karbala bleeds, she feels it is true.
The heads on lances, a slew of them,
Husayn's own tossed in his daughter's lap —
The girl, Ruqayya, a little thing.
the shock must have killed her. She mutters:

    Don't let them see you like this.
    Pull a cloth over your head, old woman.
    Dress in black. This is your family.
    One day soon, millions of them
    It's a time of idiots who kill the Prophet's family
    in his name. No one gets over it.

THE JEWISH WIVES

She who is God's Dwelling or Presence on earth…
She who when the temple fell, accompanied Israel into exile…
If two sit together and the words between them
are of Torah, it is said the Shekina is in their midst.

…Where are the women through whom the Shekina
will come, will reveal herself, will act
will decide to speak
will command to speak

Alicia Ostriker, *Return of the Mothers*

The Jewish Wives

People of the Book

And Sarah saw the son of Hagar the Egyptian, whom she had borne unto Abraham mocking (or playing). Wherefore, she said unto Abraham, "Cast out this handmaid and her son: for (her) son shall not be heir with my son, even with Isaac." ...and she (Hagar) departed and wandered in the wilderness of Beersheba. [The Holy Bible: Genesis].[78]

When Abraham had differences with his wife (Sarah), because of her jealousy of Hagar, Ishmael's mother, he took Ishmael and his mother and went away. (He left Hagar) and she called him, "Oh Abraham, to whom are you leaving us?" He replied, "I am leaving you to Allah's care." She said, "I am satisfied to be with Allah. [hadith, Ibn 'Abbas].[79]

J EWISH AND ISLAMIC accounts are the same. Sarah, the Jewish matriarch, casts out Hagar, the mother of all Muslims.[80] However, the two passages above are different in their approach to the story. In Genesis we find the bare-bones tale of Sara's jealousy and Hagar's dismissal. The hadith, however, seems more like a parable, an account of perfect surrender to God and its reward.

After all, what mother would agree to being abandoned in the desert with her child and little more? What mother can be satisfied that her God will care for all their needs? Hagar's story is the story of unquestioning self-surrender to Allah. Her son, Ishmael, is recognized as the father of all the tribes of Arabia and, and in particular, of Muhammad.[81]

Abraham, Sarah, and Hagar's story is part of the early family lore of the People of the Book. It is a cautionary tale of competition and jealousy, which was well known during the time of Muhammad, and served to highlight the grave responsibility of any prophet's wife or concubine to keep the family peace and avoid the worst possible outcome, the sundering of a family. The dignity of mutual support and sisterhood that may have occurred between these two mothers has been written out of the telling long ago.

But this is simply a tale. The story of the Prophet's Jewish wives is larger than any struggle between women in a house. It has to do with deep currents of faith and statecraft.

A recent historian provides a fresh outlook on the beleaguered rift between the Muslims and the Jews during the Prophet's life. After describing hostility between the two groups as disunity over tribal partnerships and economics, he writes that the hadiths were compiled after Arabia was almost completely Islamic, except for a minority of Jews.

> It is not surprising, therefore, that Muslim historians and theologians would have buttressed their arguments against the authorities of their time by planting their words in Muhammad's mouth. If Muhammad's biographers reveal anything at all, it is the anti-Jewish sentiments of the Prophet's biographers, not of the Prophet himself. To understand Muhammad's actual beliefs concerning the Jews and Christians of his time, one must look not to the words that chroniclers put into his mouth hundreds of years after his death, but rather to the words that God put into his mouth while he was alive... As far as Muhammad was concerned, the Jews and Christians were "People of the Book" (*ahl al-kitab*), spiritual cousins who, as opposed to the pagans and polytheists of Arabia, worshipped the same God, read the same scriptures, and shared the same moral values as his Muslim community.[82]

During the Prophet's years in Mecca, the emphasis of Islam was on monotheism. Christianity and Judaism were sister religions, mentioned in the Qur'an. The stories of all three religions, as we see above, ran parallel. However, the exile to Medina placed Muslims under pressure as an immigrant group. Now, Islam positioned itself as an Abrahamic religion with a prophet. In Medina, Muhammad took his wives exclusively from the Arab tribes: [Hafsa, daughter of 'Umar, his close friend, Umm Salama, widow of one of his generals, Zaynab, his second cousin, Umm Habiba, daughter of an Umayyad cousin, and Juwayria, daughter of the Ibn al-Mustaliq clan chief.]

As he came into his own in Medina, Muhammad was able to act inclusively. After several years there, he could take responsibility for Rayhana, a Jewish battle captive, known to history variously as his concubine and his wife.[83] She was followed into the *umma* by Safiyya, a willing convert from the enemy city of Khaybar. Both women had been brought up in Arabia as Jews, and raised to carry forward the traditions and wisdom of the mothers. The Prophet's followers were wary of the influence of the two young women from an unfamiliar tradition. The gap was ancient. The wives may not have felt the impact of Sarah's actions, since they grew up in the pagan world, yet Hagar stood for all Arab women. She was present long ago when the spring of Zamzam burst out of the desert. Hagar's separation from Prophet Abraham continues to be felt and heard:

lament for Hagar's daughters

Broken thing between
women, I hear you

grinding your teeth
cursing me.

The names of separation
are these:

the blue wastelands of sand —
the sky of icy wind —
the singing sword of water —
the unraveled carpet of famine —
a sacrificial lamb that rots —
and human death with no burial.

I, Rayhana, have

nothing but
myself here, reaching out

with Sarah's hand.

Rayhana remained on the outer edge of the community. Her marriage to Muhammad carried the pain of both the cut and the cure. These marriages tested the Muslim community by mandating, as they did, a more inclusive definition of family. But how did the two women impact Muhammad? What knowledge and understanding of Judaism did they share with him? True, both converted to Islam, but they carried with them a conscious transmission of lineage, their connection back to Abraham.

It is important to note here that there were friendly and neutral Jews living in the oasis of Medina along with the Prophet and that his alliance with them was important to the Muslims. Despite the webs of antagonism they stirred, the Jewish wives added historical depth as well as cultural breadth to the Prophet's household. These women crossed over into Islam, but the story of other Jews in Arabia started long before the seventh century.

In 70 AD, after the Romans torched the Second Temple, they slaughtered thousands of Jews then ripped apart the smoldering Holy of Holies to scrape up its melted gold. In the diaspora that followed, numbers of Jews fled into Arabia where they joined settlements like Yathrib (later Medina) and Khaybar as well as a chain of oasis centers, Petra, Fadak and Tayma, and Yemen in southern Arabia. In the centuries that followed, Arabia lay between enormous foreign powers: Persia, Rome, Byzantium, and Abyssinia. Religious, political, and economic jostling went on continually between these giants, wearying their subjects and extracting taxes from those they conquered.

Despite this rough-and-tumble atmosphere, the new Jewish immigrants adjusted and took their place among Arabs. Nomads and nobles, they lived in tents and castles, worked as armorers and jewelers, cloth merchants and tailors. They became merchants and farmers, mastered date and grape growing, and created enviable palmeries and vineyards. They even developed a special Jewish dialect of Arabic called *Yahudiyya*.

By the seventh century, Jews had prospered in this small country surrounded by large enemies and protected by a desert. The indigenous polytheistic tribes squabbled among themselves. Their law was stern; polytheistic culture was somewhat xenophobic, except relating to business. They tolerated the Jews but did not often marry them.

At this time in Medina there were many Jews, some of them were well off, none more so than the two strong extended families, the Ibn Nadir and the Ibn Qurayza. Both of these had wealth, prestige, and power; both would be important in the story of Islam. Muhammad, then, emerged as a new force free from foreign influences, an Arab, a "trustworthy" man. As such, he was called to Medina from Mecca to be a mediator between warring local clans. Upon arriving there Muhammad's chief aim must have been to gain friends so that he and his followers could move about freely without fear of being challenged. He came to conciliate and did not think he was starting a 'new' religion, but, rather, restoring and reforming the Abrahamic heritage among Jews and Christians of Arabia. This is an important distinction, and speaks to the expectation that Allah's Messenger expected to convert large numbers of Jews to Islam.

In this atmosphere, debate and discussion on the subject of religion continued between the rabbis and Muhammad. Some Jews were threatened by his interpretation of the stories of their prophets, while others were reluctant to admit that they recognized him as a prophet, since the era of prophecy had passed. Some rabbis sought excuses to engage as well as deny him. Muhammad continued to educate himself in the Abrahamic tradition and encouraged others to learn from it.[84] We must not lose sight of the fact that in the early years in Medina, Judaism represented a strong established identity and culture, while the Prophet was leader of a small nascent group, not more than one hundred people. Muhammad's greatest trial was the Muslim, Jewish, and polytheistic men who only paid him lip service. These were two-faced "allies" with weak loyalties who betrayed him. Among the followers they were known as the hypocrites, an Arabic word from the verb to "sell well" or "tunnel" *(munafiqum)*. The Qur'an has many warnings regarding them and strongly condemns their hypocrisy.[85]

the munafiqin

They smiled and said,

Great garden! And sold it to us;
the very place where moles
dug passageways through palm roots so
the ground gave way — all rocks and holes.

They smiled and said,

We follow the *Rasul!* and made a pledge;
then winked at the Meccans. Just a
wink can never break the law.

They pulled one over on us.

We called them hypocrites.
We called them two-faced to their faces.

You know how fast a rat can move?
They were in the tunneling business,
endangering us all.

Dig away, *munafiqin.* Let dirt fly!
There's no escape.
Most certainly God will *mark you out.*

In the city of Medina, some Jewish leaders saw it as only common sense to side with the powerful Quraysh against the Prophet. After all, the Quraysh bought wine, dates, and weapons from them. Two examples of switching sides were the skirmish at the well of Badr and the battle of Uhud. After Muhammad's victories, the treasonous tribes were expelled from Medina and their property confiscated. Muslim military success now allowed Muhammad to be seen as a political force with increasing power and influence. Along with this came more determined enemies. Sorcery, attempted poisoning, and the attempt to drop a rock on Muhammad from a second story were direct incidents that demonstrate the enmity directed toward Allah's Messenger by his powerful foes.

Much later Jewish history viewed Muhammad as a Jew-killer. This opinion was highlighted by the *Battle of the Trench, a* twenty-day battle. A wealthy Jewish tribe, the Qurayza, betrayed Muhammad at a crucial moment. They were neighbors who had signed "The Constitution of Mecca," a document that may have been written as a nonaggression pact among Muhammad and the various clans of Medina[86]. The battle was so closely fought that Muslims were only saved by a violent storm. In the aftermath, the defeated Qurayza expected the same leniency other treasonous groups had received from Muhammad, but this time the decision was turned over to a judge *(hakim)*, who ruled according to traditional Arab law. In the matter of treason the punishment is death for men and slavery for women and children. This was not genocide or an anti-Jewish agenda; this was customary law. After the battle, there were still thousands of Jews left in Medina, but most Qurayza men were executed and this punishment left its mark.

Rayhana

Rayhana was the first Jewish woman in Muhammad's household. After the destruction of the Qurayza, she was a captive and a widow. Her father was Zayd of the b. Nadir, her husband a Qurayza. He was called *al-hakim*, that is, one who settled disputes, a kind of judge. She had been an upper class woman who possibly spoke more than one language, and may have lived in a fortified castle or well-built house. However life was for her before, after the battle of the Trench she was a captive, marched into the courtyard with the several hundred other women and their children to be claimed as a reward by the Muslim soldiers, while the Qurayza men were led away to be executed.

Rayhana, pouring out the wine

The men were led out with their hands bound behind their backs and a space was allotted them on one side of the camp. On another side the women and children were assembled, ...The arms and armor, the garments and the household goods were collected from each fortress and all gathered together in one place. The jars of wine and fermented date juice were opened and their contents poured away.[87]

In the clamor of tossed shields and swords,
my sorrow is an armor that does not guard me.
My fingers move to touch gold bracelets,
but a rope circles my wrists.

No weapon of mine can save my clan.
In the courtyard, two men up-end
great jars of fine Arabian wine. We captives
are splashed, our feet empurpled, dark

floods the ground. The air reeks with the sour scents
of fear and fermentation. After this
last hour of the grape, there is only gore,
rust drying to brown, my father, husband, brother,

all the rest are gone—
blood stains executioners, chests and arms.
Men tell me that the "Messenger"
has chosen me, that he will send for me when

I have been washed clean. I imagine the white of linen
sheets, goat's milk, the teeth of healthy children,
creamy clouds. I consider an antelope skeleton, its beauty
when the birds have picked it dry.

Muhammad. He may have been God's Prophet. She may have believed that. But he had allowed her tribe to be destroyed, her husband to be murdered. In this tragic moment, if Rayhana turned away from him, she became the property of a lesser Muslim, a soldier. There was no other choice for her. This is an archetypal situation, repeated many times over in ancient desert culture and in any society that makes war and devalues women as "war booty." A battle captive faced life-long degradation. If her owner's wife and relatives lacked empathy and kindness, she would never be part of a family. Like a coin, she would be passed from hand to hand never knowing "home."

gold coin

I spit on happiness.

I am every conquered woman.
My young body is a gold coin on the road.
The one who sees it first will snatch it up.

I could spend years in the hand of
a hero, a cripple, or a brute.
Sometimes, for us pretty ones
the scene is grim. The men fight like dogs.

A soldier just stands there tossing
something shiny in the air and catching it.
His friends are laughing. My tongue
has the iron taste of blood. I stare at the road,

Whatever the outcome — I'll belong to some man.

As Muhammad's legal property, she began with slave status. Delivered first to the house of Muhammad's aunt, Salma, she would undergo waiting the ritual menstrual cycle that assured the tribe a captured woman had not conceived from her former partner. Then she was taken to Muhammad. And what could he say after all her trials that would make her feel safe? How could he get her to talk to him, much less be a willing partner in sex? What would cause her to share her Jewish traditions or adapt to her new husband's religion?

The Jews count matriarchy as the vessel that carries the link to Abraham. For Rayhana to convert would be a drastic change. She must then pray toward Mecca instead of Jerusalem. The Sabbath would no longer be the sacred day. How could these things be? And yet, she did convert and in the hadith we find that the Prophet was aware of her conversion, even as it happened: "[Muhammad] heard the sound of sandals behind him and said, 'This is Tha'laba b. Sa'ya coming to give me the good news of Rayhana's acceptance of Islam', and he came up to announce the fact."

She converted. She became his wife. These are the words of Rayhana: "When I became Muslim, the Messenger of Allah set me free and married me and gave me a dower...." The wedding took place in the home of Umm al-Mundhir in 628.[88] She had none of her people around her. Most of the wives may have wanted little to do with Rayhana, since they considered her people traitors. Her life as Muhammad's wife was not easy.

Muhammad's sigh

Hello, dry lava rock. Scalded, pitted, burned black.
My name is Rayhana.
Hello, shocked, mute, and crumpled.

She was thinking: *This is extinction.*

On his way to see her he was thinking: *woman, perfume, and prayer.*
It occurred to him: *Rayhana* means
"the extremely fragrant woman."

He was the Prophet.
He went and stood beside her.
He breathed in.

Then he sighed and she felt it happen;
that lava melted and hurried back inside the mountain.

It still hurt to smile.
Like any change it takes awhile to be your self again.

"She had a husband whom she loved and honored. She said, 'No one will replace him.' She was very beautiful."[89] Rayhana's name means "extremely fragrant," and Muhammad loved perfume. She was his now wife. It was more than likely she held the tradition of the Torah, as well as customs and the spirit of *midrash,* and may have shared them with the Prophet. Would he have heard a Jewish woman speak of these things before? Probably not. When he spent an evening with her, there was time for exchange. Assuming she felt safe and cared for by him, that she began to heal from the terrible trauma, she might have been engaged in good-natured debates. She possibly contributed to Muhammad's understanding of the *Shekina* (*Sakina* –Ar.), defined as "She-Who-is-God's Presence, tranquil experience," and the essence of the High, Holy days. To Muslim historians, this could be an appalling notion that might not fit into their concept of the traditions (*sunna*) of the Prophet. Whether she had friends in the community of the other wives, we'll never know. No other reports have survived. She died before Muhammad, and was buried in the Baqi' cemetery with his deceased wives and family.

What we do know is that the animosity that came out of the torn family of Abraham was profound and felt by both Arabs and Jews. Hatred would have covered cultural shame.

> *There's no way to change without touching the space at the center of everything.*
>
> Chana Bloch

In her own way, Rayhana bravely entered the "tent of Sarah and Hagar" and the steps she took toward Islam smoothed the way for Safiyya, Muhammad's second Jewish wife.

Safiyya b. Huyayy

Safiyya was from Khaybar, the wife of a general who beat her.[90] Khaybar was a town with many wealthy Jews, vast palmeries, and military presence. The rulers and power brokers had a strong desire to get rid of Muhammad. Persia was their ally, so they never imagined being defeated. One night Safiyya had a dream:

Safiyya's cat

Husband, Kinanah, wake up!

> The moon —
> > how can I tell you such a dream! —
>
> it rose over Medina, then
> floated to our city and fell into my lap.
>
> > Dare I speak of this?
> The moon curled up
> next to my belly like a milk-white cat.
> We were close all night.
>
> > Kinanah raged and struck me.

Shut the night curtains! It is forbidden!

What? Dreaming?

The dream means you desire Muhammad, my enemy,
and the enemy of your father!

> I could die for the light
> over the rim of this dream.

My face is torn. Stars keep knocking on the roof
all night. I am under their eyes.

I run into the outside dark barefoot in search of a cat.

Soon after Safiyya's dream, an overconfident Khaybar fell to Allah's Messenger. The story of the woman with a dream got Muhammad's attention. He had her brought to him and asked her the dream and about her willingness to embrace Islam. She answered that she chose Allah and his Messenger over freedom and returning to her people.

Unlike the grieving and cautious Rayhana, Safiyya felt she belonged with Muhammad and converted immediately, still wearing the marks of her husband's abuse. After she demonstrated she was not with child, Muhammad married the small, lovely-looking girl while he was returning from battle in Khaybar to Medina.

in the tent

When the Messenger of Allah consummated the marriage with Safiyya, Abu Ayyub spent the night at the door of the Prophet...with his sword." [91]

Before it happened, I waited,
smelled men's sweat,
listened to one soldier brag
how he might kill me—
if I harmed Muhammad, or
to insure I wouldn't.

That night my bridegroom
slept with me on a ram skin,
his cheek on my hair
while, in the dark, a man
crouched in the doorway
ghost moon on his sword

calmly calibrating my life
against *the Rasul's.*

If I die this hour, let this be my eulogy:
Remember
the-girl-with-the-softest-kiss,
the bride with her pale throat
cut by error.
Remember
the bride who died silent,
so as not to wake Muhammad.

Or perhaps if I die let them say:
Remember the new wife
who feigned sleep,
struck out at   the assassin
with a shout and a kick
to save herself
from injustice.

Meanwhile this is my long night's prayer:
God of all the universes —
whatever your name is—
I'm caught by fists of early light,
the fast release of the well rope and the music
of my new husband's laugh.
Let me live.

As they entered Medina to a joyful welcome, Muhammad took Safiyya onto his camel and wrapped her in his cloak for all to see she was his wife. In this dramatic moment, he visibly honored his new Jewish wife, and in doing so, shook the hornet's nest of prejudices in the *umma*. With Safiyya at his side, it is likely he hoped that his community could learn more about the people of the book. But they got off to a difficult start:[92]

Safiyya's fall

They run alongside the camel, hungry
for Muhammad home from the rout;
townspeople, his family, all shouting,
as-salamu 'alaykum! When his animal stumbles,
the woman rolls out of the Prophet's mantle,
her head and shoulders in the gray dirt.

What they see of his new Jewish wife is meant
for his eyes. They keep on looking at the unconcealed

woman, spilled out, bruised. They stare at her ankle, cheek,
leg, shoulder, arm, neck, all the shock of luxurious curls,
at the trickle of blood down her arm. Safiyya will
spend the rest of her life dusting herself off, getting up.

again and again as if tripped by the shadow —
Sarah's words to Hagar — I'll stay, you have to go.

Almost from the start, Safiyya was on the defensive, at odds with the other wives. 'A'isha reports that when Safiyya's camel fell ill on a journey; Zaynab refused to lend her another, saying to Muhammad, "I… give to that Jewess?" Muhammad was displeased, as the story goes, and didn't visit Zaynab for three months.[93] Imagine how popular Safiyya must have been with the other wives. When Muhammad was suffering from his final illness, the wives gathered and Safiyya spoke: "By Allah, O Messenger of Allah, I wish it was I who was suffering instead of you!" It is said that one or more of the women made an audible expression of disgust. Muhammad looked at them and said, "Whoever did that, rinse out your mouth! By Allah, she spoke truthfully."[94] Could the tone of anti-Semitism that runs through the hadith be a cover for the other wives' jealousy? How must this life have been for the Jewish newcomer?

It is said that Safiyya gave her heirloom gold earrings to Fatima, daughter of the Prophet.[95] What happened to the incidents marking their friendship or sisterhood? Where are the antidotes that point to Safiyya explaining the Old Testament stories contained in the Qur'an, on behalf of the women and children of the *umma*? Some Moroccan Sufis teach that she was just that — a teacher for those women. It is likely that any praises for her were among the hundreds of stories that came to be known as "weak hadith," weeded out by later scholars and lost forever. Since there are no formal examples of her sisterhood with the other wives, here is an imagined interview with Safiyya, conducted in present time:

interview with Safiyya

How was it to be Jewish with all the Muslim wives?

I belonged. I only happened to be Jewish and an enemy. He took
me. I was in the *umma,* inner circle. Listen, once we all were pagan,
Christian, Jew, in those days, every one of us, a convert.

The histories say the other wives avoided you—.

They write as if they were there, a hundred years after the founding.
Imagine! Who remembers? So historians find tales to build a case on
exclusion of the newer wives like me.

But Zaynab b. Jahsh hated you, didn't she?

Well, Zaynab refused me a camel. But only because I borrowed her
hand-stitched dress and left it at a caravan stop. I can't blame her,
can you?

What about 'A'isha turning on you and your family?

'A'isha challenged all of us even her husband, the Prophet! I didn't
take it personally. The hadith are sometimes out of context! Listen,
we stuck together. Those were rough times, and strangers elbowed
in to influence Muhammad through his wives. It drove us crazy. We
fought and bickered, over him, over spoils. We weren't best friends,
but we were too wise for anti-Semitism. Jew and Christian, we have
the same God.

So you were established in the umma, like the Arabs?

There was a pecking order as in any harem, but there we each had
different strengths. No one told you I knew languages, did they—
Hebrew, Arabic, and Aramaic? I told stories from the Torah to the
children, let them question, like a *midrash,* and I practiced Islam, too.
Later scholars made up stories to make every Jew look bad.

Look in this mirror. There I am, *Mother of the Faithful;* faithful myself,
to Allah's Messenger, faithful to His Message. You are in there too!
Part of a mighty time!

MARIYA, FROM AMONG THE CHRISTIANS

so knowing
what is known?

that it is more difficult
than faith
to serve only one calling
one commitment
one devotion
in one life.

Lucille Clifton, *gloria mundi*

Mariya, from among the Christians

Muhammad and Christianity

locution

Hear her speak in Coptic; a splash
of Nile water in each phrase, and why not
kitchen Greek—learned at her yaya's knee?
And after, listen to her message in Aramaic.
That talk is coin for diplomats and travelers,
a purse to ease Mariya into Arabic,
protect from word-danger, sweeten her welcome.

WHEN MARIYA THE Copt came to Muhammad as a gift from the leader of the Egyptian Coptic Church, what languages did she speak? She would have carried the message of Christianity to the *umma* — that is if she spoke languages other than Coptic. Could Mariya even speak a language Muhammad understood? If she knew Aramaic, she might have learned enough Arabic to be of counsel to the Prophet, sharing information about Jesus, as well as her grasp of Greek philosophy. This would have been useful to him.

In the thinking of many Muslims and Christians of the twenty-first century, Christianity and Islam share little other than a common ancestor, Abraham. It is nearly inconceivable to them that Muhammad would say, "I am the nearest of all the people to the son of Mary, and all the prophets are paternal brothers...."[96]

The Prophet Muhammad first connected with Christianity as a young man traveling with his uncle, Abu Talib. While they were in Syria, a Christian monk recognized the young Muhammad and told his uncle, "Great things lie ahead of him, so take him back quickly to his country."[97] Later when Muhammad broke the idols in the Ka'ba, he is said to have spared the fresco of Mary and Jesus on the wall inside of the Ka'ba.[98] Other Christians also recognized him. A Christian bishop from Najran, south of Mecca, named Abu Haritha, confided to his brother that Muhammad was the awaited Prophet.[99] The Prophet was comfortable enough with Christian Abyssinia to send a large group of his followers there in the course of the upheavals in Mecca. During the Muslims' sojourn, the Christian *Negus*, the emperor of Abyssinia, was not only sympathetic, but swore allegiance to

Muhammad and endorsed Islam.[100] Hadith mentioning Jesus are positive, for example: "If anyone testifies that none has the right to be worshipped but Allah alone, who has no partners, and that Muhammad is His Slave and his Apostle and that Jesus is Allah's Slave and his Apostle... Allah will admit him into Paradise with the deeds that he hath done, even if those deeds were few."[101]

How could this open spirit have been so totally lost? The Abyssinians as well as Christians in southern and central Arabia were friendly, while the tribes in the north under Byzantine influence became hostile. This drew a negative response from Muslims from 630 on. For Muhammad, it was Christian doctrine that disappointed, while he continued to honor Mary and Jesus.

As Christianity grew and spread, so did internal dissension. One point of deadly debate among those in the Byzantine Empire, specifically with the Egyptian Copts, had to do with how the church formulated the message that Jesus was God-in-man, setting off accusations of heresy to those who denied that belief. Muhammad and his followers saw the controversy as "ascribing partners to God" *(shirk),* that is, something they had no stomach for. The hadith using the word "Christian" became invariably negative, with emphasis on the unacceptable message of Jesus as Son of God. History does not clearly indicate how closely the Companions were acquainted with the Christian beliefs prior to the conquest of Mecca. They may have thought that most Christians regarded Jesus merely as a prophet. The early Muslims did not understand the principle of atonement. The theology of a Holy Spirit with God the Father and the Son was unrecognized and would have been thought strange. Muslim understanding of Christianity was limited to "Prophet Jesus," and that view does not seem to have changed over the centuries.

Egypt, the birthplace of Mariya, mother of Prophet Muhammad's son Ibrahim, was a thoroughly Christian country. Although the Chalcedon Council of 451 had failed to unify Egyptian Christians, ascetics were an institution in every area of life. By the time of the Prophet, Coptic Christianity was austere, with fasting over two hundred days a year. The sacrament of communion was seen as a direct connection with the God-Christ. With monotheism, the Copts had completely turned aside from their roots in ancient Egyptian culture and religion. The pharaohs and scribes were buried with their mighty monuments and their gods were reduced to demons and harmful spirits. Just before 618, the Persians destroyed some 600 Coptic monasteries along the Nile, and then conquered the international jewel, the city of Alexandria. Byzantine Emperor Heraclius, in 627, drove the Persians from Egypt and somewhat later appointed the tyrant Cyrus of Alexandria as patriarch. Some sources say Cyrus arrived after Mariya had gone to Medina. Earlier, the Coptic patriarch, Benjamin, fled south to Upper Egypt and pressed for unity among Christian factions. Was he the real *Muqawqis* (Egyptian bishop) who wisely sent Mariya and her sister Shirin to Prophet Muhammad? The era between the Persian and the Muslim occupations is so historically confused, no one seems to know. Although she emerged in Alexandria as a young girl, most details of her life are speculation and her very existence is challenged by the *Encyclopedia of Islam*.[102]

Mariya, the Copt, was born at the beginning of the seventh century, in Upper Egypt. Her heritage may have included Greek relatives, as there were many from Greece in Egypt at that time, and Greek was a commonly spoken language.[103] Older Islamic sources say she was a pretty slave girl, but they do not mention whether she was educated, trained in the feminine arts, languages, or diplomacy. What can be said is that growing up in Alexandria she would have been exposed to a cosmopolitan Mediterranean culture with echoes of its ancient greatness.

However, by 618 the Persian army had swept into the city after conquering the Holy Land. These Zoroastrian soldiers had little respect for Christianity, or any monotheism for that matter. Many Alexandrians perished in a massacre. Perhaps Mariya and her sister Shirin lost one or both parents at this time. In that case, the girls would have sought refuge in the church or with what was left of their family's political connections. In either new home, they would have been educated. Also, their status as orphans would explain why the two girls were sent away to Arabia, rather than married to Egyptian men.

Egypt was a ripe plum sought after and conquered over centuries by the Romans, Byzantines, Persians, and finally the Muslims during 'Umar's rule. The well-being of Egypt rested with the care of its conquerors. The powerful job of feeding Rome or Constantinople was the result of enormous harvests, crops that came from the once-a-year flooding of the Nile farmlands by rain in the depths of Africa. In the middle of a burning summer, for three months, the Nile rose over its bed and transformed the country. Uncertainty about the annual rise of the river was mixed with relief and celebration when the flooding came without damage, then receded leaving a wide green area from the heart of Africa to the Mediterranean Sea.

Mariya leaves Egypt for Medina

May 11, 628 Muhammad sent a letter to the *Muqawqis* of Egypt inviting him to become a Muslim. Although we cannot be sure who this ruler or bishop was, Egypt sent Muhammad a gracious reply. Sometime between April 30 and May 11, 629 a gift caravan arrived in Medina from the *Muqawqis*. In it were "...Mariya, her sister Shirin, a thousand gold coins, twenty fine robes, the mule Duldul, and the donkey 'Ufayr, or Ya'fur as well as a very old eunuch called Mabur."[104] Mariya left Egypt for a land without Christianity or the Nile. Maybe she was caught up in the spirit of adventure. Or perhaps she held the big picture, with love for Egypt and few illusions of its realities.

between

Can I still speak the old words,
remember the childhood phrases that calmed me,
the Coptic that calls up my church and land?

In the name of our lord Jesus Christ
praise to the hundred and fifty holy fathers who
introduced the worship of God in three:
Father, Son, and Holy Spirit

and: praise to the river-mother of Egypt
                        the flood season (*Thout* to *Kioahk*)
                        brown.
                        the planting and growing time (*Tobe* to *Paremonde*)
                        green.

the Holy Spirit was abundant among the priests
their hands and tongues and thoughts were pure
and peace prevailed in the churches
and infidelity and heresy were driven out

                        harvest and festivals (*Pachons* to *Mesore*)
                        golden.

How the church prospered. How jealous Satan was. What came to us
Roman, Byzantine, Persian; conquest, conquest, conquest
a nest in the arch of the pulled-down monastery,

> upstream, the harvest serves our conquerors,

downstream, we fast to serve our Lord.[105]

Imagine the caravan on its way from Egypt, with its guides, guards, and
camels laden with supplies and gifts, and led by one of Muhammad's diplomats, Hatib b. Abi Balt'a. The overland journey would have taken at least
a couple of weeks, traveling east across the delta, in the footsteps of Mary,
Joseph and Jesus returning from Egypt, then across the Sinai where they
met either the Syria-Medina road or the route along the eastern shore of the
Red Sea. Imagine that journey, the dust and heat, the creak of the *howdahs*,
the sisters' small voices speaking Coptic or Greek amidst the guttural hub-
bub of Arab phrases, and the bustle of slaves and drivers.

   During the journey south, hadith tells us that the sisters converted to
Islam. Was that true? If so, Mariya would not have been a "slave" girl, as
she was sometimes called. She and her sister were People of the Book. Was
that enough to safeguard them? Religion was one with group identity, and
since they carried the nationality of "Egyptian" into Medina, that conversion could ease the women's status and protection. We may never know
their true status because of the deliberate ambiguity surrounding Mariya.
How can we have the name of the mule that came with her to Arabia —
Dudul — and lack so many fundamental facts about the woman who was
to become the mother of Prophet Muhammad's son?

Mariya's needle

I am Egyptian linen unrolled into the desert
I stitch the fine fabric of my house and a garden onto Medina;
darning the moth-hole of impatient men
reweaving Arabia wool by my own design.
I'm good with a needle.

Wind snaps the howdah curtains, the platform
dips with each step of the camel. I bend to pick up
my mending. When I lean back, my comfort is
my Greek grandmother's cushion.
I know once more her wise hands against my neck

Beyond the yellow drapes, sharp thorn bush and sand —
I yearn for green.

It is easier for a camel to go
through the eye of a needle than for a
rich man to enter the Kingdom of God."
Jesus said that. I am not rich, although I ride
with my eyeful of tears, crying and threading.
What can He mean: *to enter The Kingdom of God?*

Mariya's Arabian life begins with her moving through the desert, between countries and between religions, accompanied by people who did not speak her language. Imagine then the sisters' relief, and their trepidation, after those long, hot days on the trail, as the city of the Prophet came into view.

When the caravan reached Medina, Allah's Messenger chose Mariya and presented her sister Shirin to Hasan b. Thabit.[106] Mariya's relationship to Muhammad is described by most sources as concubine or slave. This description was in line with contemporary usage. Besides marriage, there was one sort of relationship between women and men in which the woman belonged to the man and was, to use a denigrating phrase, his property. Unlike his Arab and Jewish wives, she had her own house with a garden called *al-'Aliyya*. He also "…set up a screen for her," an act which usually implied the status of wife. Since we are told Mariya had converted to Islam, it is possible that the Prophet married her.[107] If he did so, this would have made her the only foreign woman honored by marriage. Allah's Messenger would have been close to sixty years old when he met Mariya. He was nearly at the peak of his life's work. His activities and the words that flowed from his mouth had begun a revolution of God-consciousness. It would be natural for him to honor this Christian, Islamic convert with marriage. Historical memory, including the hadith of the other wives, stubbornly views her as a concubine, clearly an outsider.

Mariya

I am the one-woman-peacekeeping bride from Egypt,
Most will call me "concubine," though he will call me
names of flowers and flowing water.
The Copts will remember me for generations.

But her life cannot have been easy. From all indications, she remained a distant figure, passing her time with her sister and Muhammad. At one point, her Coptic servant was nearly killed by 'Ali, who responded to a rumor about a man's comings and goings in Mariya's house and went to confront him, only to discover he was a eunuch. Umm Salama and Umm Habiba, having lived among the Abyssinian Christians, may have known how to make their new sister feel welcome, but this relationship would have been complicated since all the sources emphasize that Muhammad was very taken with curly-haired Mariya and gave her an inordinate amount of his time. 'A'isha comments that she and the other wives were jealous of the Coptic woman. "This was because she was beautiful. The Messenger of God admired her… The Messenger of God spent most of the day and night with her so that we (the other wives) became preoccupied with her. She became alarmed. He moved her to *al-'Aliyya* [the house with the garden]. He used to visit there. It was hard on us. Then God gave him a son by her, and we were deprived of that."[108]

why they complain about the Egyptian

The man Muhammad
does not reason as
he strolls then stops, moves
again among the lifted blossoms,
violet, white. Only filtered sunlight
and the shaded moon touch this bed
of impossible plants
meant to grow in cooler ground.

In all Arabia only in this garden,
the Phlox Maculata, immaculate flowers.

Only in Mariya's garden
where a walk on summer evenings
lingers, as his lips linger on her skin,
and may keep a man late at his prayers.

Relations between Mariya and the wives reached a theatrical pitch as we see from the following hadith. Hadith tells us: "The Messenger of Allah was alone with his slave girl Mariya in Hafsa's room. The Prophet came out and she (Hafsa) was sitting at the door. She said, 'Messenger of Allah! In my room and on my day!' She said, 'I will not accept it without you swearing an oath to me.' So he said, 'By Allah, I will never touch her'."[109]

Muhammad knew how volatile Hafsa could be and asked her not to discuss what happened, but Hafsa was not a woman known for restraint and complained about it to the others. But then Muhammad received a verse from the Qur'an, so he withdrew his promise: *O Prophet, why does thou out of a desire to please [one or another of] thy wives, impose [on thyself] a prohibition of something that God has made lawful to thee?.... [O wives of the Prophet], were he to divorce any of you, his Sustainer might well give him in your stead spouses better than you — women who surrender themselves unto God, who truly believe... [Q. 66:1–5].*

Muhammad was disturbed by the feminine chaos brought about by jealousy. Mariya seemed to be a catalyst for change, igniting the sparking tension between the women living with Allah's Messenger. There was also bickering about the new wealth that came from the spoils of battle. He needed time to reflect and receive guidance, so he withdrew to a porch above the mosque for a month. The women were afraid he had divorced them.

excerpt from on the porch

Muhammad climbs to the porch and pulls the ladder up.
He carries his gear,   water skin, blanket, tooth stick.
Below, where the women chatter,   relentless as cicadas,

caught in faction and backtalk, chit-chat and story
telling,   the place is struck with unnatural quiet.
When will he come down?   The wives are waiting...

When he came down, he brought a message that the women must rededicate themselves to the Message he carried and to cooperation. The wives agreed to a life focused on Allah. It was then they may have begun to be called, "Mothers of Islam." Mariya's life would have been more peaceful, although she still might have been homesick. She was far from the lush Nile. Her new home was surrounded by desert and lava fields. Plants and flowers were comforting, but she had few confidants. Her Egyptian upbringing made her odd in the Arab culture. Her special foods, her knowledge of Greek thought, and Christian culture set her apart. It would be natural for Mariya to have deep respect and reverence for Mary, Mother of Jesus. With

that in mind, this imagined story sets the stage for Muhammad's famous
words in Mecca.

in her garden Mariya has a vision

Not the trespassing goats,
nor the goat-boys in pursuit, slipping on garden mud and fallen figs;
not their shouts, not the bleat and baah,
not the scuffle that brought me running to the tree

Not the figs the boys snatched and stuffed their cheeks,
not my sister,
Shirin, yelling at them from the house.

It was the blue
crossing blue in cool air; a vision
of Mary, robed in indigo,
that lit the wall by the tree.

That stopped the herd, until
not a hoof flew, the wispy tips of every tail
were still. Ears forward in the quiet —
listening with me for Mary's voice
a little rainfall of light:

Wash everything except what is under my hands.
                              Then she was gone.

"Listen," I said to Muhammad that night, and I told him.

Later, in Mecca,
when he stood before the pale painting
of Mary and the child, Jesus, he hid it with his hands
and said to 'Uthman:

Wash everything except what is under my hands.
Let Maryam and Isa b. Maryam remain.

Some mornings, I think of the goats. How they want
to eat the whole garden. Stand
on their back legs snapping branches,
pull down every leaf, every fig.[110]

Could there be a connection between Mariya's Christian roots and Muhammad's wish to keep the fresco of Mary and Jesus from being destroyed? When Muhammad broke the idols, Mariya would either have just become a mother or would soon be giving birth. She had conceived soon after her arrival in Medina. This would have been the time for Muhammad to have learned about and discussed Christian topics as she was absorbing the teachings of Islam and her impending motherhood. No wonder they spent so much time together!

She gave birth to a son, Ibrahim, named for the Prophet who is respected by all the People of the Book. It would have made Muhammad deeply happy to have fathered a son and added to his joy of being a grandfather. By birthing a son, Mariya achieved what no other woman in the Prophet's life was able to do. But the joy didn't last; Ibrahim died at eighteen months, three days before an eclipse that occurred on January 27, 632. Muhammad died a few months later.

outliving him

He's the one,
the mama's boy who
buries his face in her skirts.
He's Ibrahim, shouting
Abba! as his father arrives.
He's the toddler who can squat
and hug the white goat or kiss
Shirin as she mashes ripe dates.

This is before the fever,
the coughing, and convulsions;
a short time before
the whimpering begins.

But when his voice stops,
it seems to his aunt
that the Cool Hands of God,
appear like water to float him
through more burning hours,
and more hours still, until
he's limp as sleep and ashen.

Mariya does not let go of her dead child.
She won't answer. She's in a heap

repeating her baby-name for him,
staring at toe-smudges in the dust
of one small-size sandal.

Shirin is running down the hill to find Muhammad.

Ibn 'Abbas commented, "When the mother of Ibrahim gave birth, the Messenger of Islam said, 'Her son has freed her.'"[111] This means she has greater status. But as mentioned, there is no certain agreement that he married her, although she was buried where the wives were, in the Baqi' cemetery. It is written that Ibrahim's birth "freed Mariya" and insured she would be remembered as a "Mother of Islam." The birth of a son of the Prophet celebrated Egypt's gift to Islam by honoring the Coptic Christians: Allah's Messenger said: "Take care of the Copts. They have protection and kinship...Isma'il b. Ibrahim was from them and the mother of Ibrahim, the son of the Prophet, was from them."[112] Mariya followed Muhammad and her son in death, five years later.

It is more than likely that the tag "slave girl" was given her by those with some degree of xenophobia, jealousy, and suspicion; the ones who wished to lessen her stature. Later, hadith historians selected what remains of her story at a time when Christianity and Judaism were rejected by Islam. But what may be most striking about Mariya is the strong possibility that this woman from Egypt — in her role as diplomat sent from her people to keep them safe — may have actually shared with Muhammad knowledge about the political, cultural, and scriptural customs of her country; a place rich with history and connection to the Mediterranean communities, and charged with a profound contemplative form of Christianity. This is speculation. But we do know this: Mariya's immersion in Islam worked as a blessing and protection for her people. The Copts paid a small tax to the *Caliphate* for the next four hundred years, and in return their church and its Christians inside Egypt were respected by Muslim rule until the 12th century, when Egypt became a Muslim country. The Coptic Church refers to Mariya as The Prophet of Islam's "Egyptian Wife." They mention the special tax of protection and Muhammad's words, uttered more than once: "Be kind to the Copts for they are your protégés and kith and kin."[113]

THE OTHER WIVES

SAWDA

ZAYNAB B. KHUZAYMA

HAFSA

JUWAYRIYYA

UMM HABIBA

ASMA'

MAYMUNA

Soon we will descend the widows' descent in the memory fields
and raise our tent to the final winds: blow, for the poem to live, and blow
on the poem's road.

Mamoud Darwish, *Here the Birds' Journey Ends*

The Other Wives

E ACH WOMAN in this chapter was born into a social system that
sustained numerous communities of differing beliefs. A woman
naturally followed the beliefs she was born into. Tolerance of other
religions was practiced. The word "pagan" was used by the Christians to
describe any religion other than Christianity or Judaism. In this pre-Muslim
time, belief in a creator god *al-ilah* (the god) was present in the background.
Active faith centered on these main divine mediators: al-Kutba and Hubal,
as well as the three goddesses, Allat, al-'Uzza, and Manat.[114] There were said
to be a total of three hundred and sixty deities in the Ka'ba. The mother
in this poem prayed regularly to the goddess. Her primary concern for her
daughter was that she preserve the transmission of feminine knowledge that
supports sound decisions; so she would guide her family with wisdom and
not fall sway to a man's rules. A matriarch might speak as this poem does:

Mother-in Law of Muhammad

My daughter stood so near the storm
of God's Words it seemed to me
her mother-tongue might wash away.

New spangled language pummeled her
and smeared her eyes, a downpour
of what she welcomed: *Allah's Grace.*

I had come north to see her — a bride again —
her back stretched tall, while palms
sprawled lower with each holy squall.

We lugged well water, boiled rough soup. She
lived his life now. I had to think it through;
in this austerity, children seemed unlikely.

I thought we thought alike, that she saw
life as I did. What to make of her surrender
so rich with upwash, so poor in conversation.

I never asked her how it felt to be his
one-of-many. I held my tongue — he was
her port in calm and tempest —as I left

pressed coins inside her sewing chest.
At home I eat my girl child's favorite dish.
I eat for her. Savor wine sauce

with the lamb and Damascus herbs.
I'm glad her man is good and values
a smart woman. Pray to the goddess

my neighbors won't kill him.
I take her life as fact. As we say:
None but a mule denies its family.

Sawda: the stamp of approval

In the year 619, Muhammad lost both Khadija and his protector, Uncle Talib, the head of the clan. Not only was he bereft, he needed help at home with his two unmarried daughters, Umm Kulthum and Fatima. His community looked to him for guidance, while townspeople opposed his new ideas. That same year, Sawda, a woman who had been in the *umma* since the beginning, came home to Mecca from exile in Abyssinia with her husband and became a widow. By the time Sawda's months of mourning finished, Muhammad was persuaded by close friends to take a wife and that she was a good choice. Sawda was a woman of maturity and steadiness with proven housewifely abilities. They were married.

One night, in the year 622, as a group of conspirators approached Muhammad's house bent on murdering him, they heard the sounds of women, most likely Sawda, Umm Kulthum, Fatima, and Umm Ayman, their servant. They might have been laughing or outraged about some household slight: they were in a lively discussion. The plotters changed their plan when they realized that to raid that woman's gathering would be to shatter the potent social taboo against violating woman's privacy. They decided to wait for Muhammad outside and, while they slept, he escaped without detection.

laughter in the dark of the moon

*If they broke into the house "...their names would be forever held
in dishonor among the Arabs, because they had violated the privacy of women."*[115]

                                                            Martin Lings

          for Asha

A home needs the protection of mirth,
the guffaws of laughing women, to fortify
the walls and windows. Giggling

finds its own way through the doors,
into the ears of the assassins waiting outside,
where a man thumbs his knife, another

squats there impatient, until they are all caught
by that raucous mood. One imagines
his sister and her silly friends inside,

so he sheathes the weapon. By now,
the women are holding their sides, yelling,
stop for the love of God, I can't take it!

Two of the assailants grow sheepish.
One is trying not to laugh, but his shoulders bounce
anyway. A fourth hits at him with a stick.

Whoops of delight roll into the street
while men in dark clothes
scuffle under the Prophet's window.

Peace on earth does not depend on quiet.

Allah's Messenger escaped and fled to Medina. There he directed the building of the mosque and apartments for his family. Sawda arrived with Fatima, Umm Kulthum, and Umm Ayman a bit later and would probably have
supervised the arrangement of the first Medina household. Within a year or
so, the very young bride, 'A'isha, joining the household would have lived in
a room near Sawda's own. She recalled: "Never did I find any woman more
loving to me than Sawda. I wished I could be exactly like her."[116]

     Yet 'A'isha's mischief often found a target in Sawda's gullible side. She
teased Sawda by telling her that the false prophet had appeared *(dajjal)*. And
Sawda, who was extremely frightened of the *dajjal*, hurried to hide, while

'A'isha and Hafsa burst with laughter. When they ran to tell Muhammad, he
rescued his fearful wife, who was 'covered with cobwebs.'

There seem to be few physical descriptions of the Wives translated
in the hadith. Safiyya is mentioned as small, while Zaynab, Juwayriyya,
and Mariya are described as beautiful. 'A'isha said, of Sawda, she was "a
slow woman." This could mean she was heavy, and a weighty woman often
meant a well-off man. Thieves and hypocrites might mark her as a target
for goods or information. 'Umar urged Muhammad to seclude his woman,
using for his reason the fact that Sawda was "a large woman recognized at a
distance and even at night."[117]

up until the Day Of Rising

Sawda dreamed Muhammad
stepped on her neck; His instep
soft, the pressure firm
and it meant *yes,* this seal, this stamp
of God's Prophet. They say
that his grief that year ran deep
his need, a woman who could
keep his house and school his girls —

the widow Sawda?
    Oh Lord, she thought, *am I to marry such as he!*

Dawn does not come twice
to wake any woman
but once she woke, Sawda came
to rule his hearth,
the big, unmigratory wife
with the sloshy walk. She left a wake.
Her footprints pressed down
deep into the soil when she walked out.
She'd puff her cheeks with effort,
find a doorframe she could lean on.

Her nights-with-Muhammad
lessened, moved to storage,
and were abandoned to 'A'isha
as she lagged behind.
The word *divorce* swam
in her brain; she feared

a life apart from him.
As for her faith, she held it,
made ablution from a pail,
drew her wet hands over her hair,
but bowing down? Well then,
her knees might fail her
or a nosebleed start. She trembled,
sucked on dates and rolled her eyes:

I have no urge for husbands, but I want Allah
to raise me up as your wife on the Day of Rising.[118]

Muhammad laughed. He saw
she was on her laborious way up,
    and who would wish to stop her?

As it happened, Sawda lived twenty-two years after the death of the Prophet. How did she, or any of the wives for that matter, cope with this terrible loss? Muhammad's death would have sent waves of shock, confusion, deep sadness and a kind of vertigo through the whole community. Each wife had lost her husband, intimate friend, and spiritual guide. In a culture where the collective is so important, and the individual is secondary, loneliness is rare. Despite the collective grieving, it is very likely that each wife felt herself to be alone. Conversely, the men who took over the administration and guidance of the community would have seen each of these women as part of a highly honored collective, known as the Mothers of the Faithful. Gone was the man who could read each individual heart and bring magnetism and kindness to every encounter. Before, they had practiced a kind of self-protective seclusion, shielding them from the bright light of Muhammad's popular appeal. But now, they may have found themselves directed to stay inside. Could the seclusion phrase in the Qur'an have a larger meaning? What if "abide quietly in your homes" could be translated "abide there among those who command respect and have a God-inspired peace of mind?"[119] Scholarship supports this translation. Each time a wider view was squeezed like this, an important message was distorted. Each of these widows held a powerful presence, both collectively and individually. It would have been important for them to share their stories, to be an example to others.

news

The Vault of Heaven is closed and draped in black. A sign:
reads: *Out of Service Since Muhammad's Death.*
"I heard this at the well," Maymuna tells us. Her pail is dry.

No stars or moon appeared last night — only the-bug-eyed-wind
blew in, and simple tasks come round again,
bewilder us. I check to see that someone hauled in water —

Sawda says, "— God help us, no girl can be his new wife now!
'A'isha, Hafsa, Safiyya and the rest are pulled-up flowers —
cannot wed again. My one night's vision of Muhammad,

in a dream, was like ten-thousand nights of bliss.
I've stayed his wife, although I am fat and old. Such loss!
I cry until I'm hoarse." The young ones sob as well, "We miss

those happy nights!" Umm Ayman, once his baby nurse,
just moans: "Alas! There's no more news from heaven now" only a hiss
of unimagined oil, the roar of war. Dreams come to us

from an impending time of reckless violence and fear.
When night is done, so others may hear us, Prophet's wives
wake up! and nudge Remembrance from its vault — the heart.[120]

Zaynab b. Khuzayma, mother of the poor

In 624, during the early days of Medina, Muhammad married a generous
woman named Zaynab b. Khuzaymah, known as "Mother of the Poor."
She was a widow whose husband had been killed at the Battle of Badr. The
sad fact was that many men died on the battlefield or from sickness leaving
women and children alone.

the other Zaynab

I called for her, not expecting an answer
but because her impression—
like a fingerprint on glass—
was missing from these tales,
her finger sugared with the juice of
a fresh apricot, the one that pressed
for a second or two on that glass mentioned above,

that is, if there was glass at all,
or a rough cup or a heavy Phoenician goblet
or a pane from Yemen, fitted
into the earthen wall
of some Meccan mansion, tinted
maybe a pale rose color,
like the blush on an apricot,
or the heat in her cheek the first time
Muhammad took her hand.

In seventh century Arabia, one solution to a widow's distress was polygamy, the other option was to return to her parents, if they were living. Muhammad set an example for his people of caring for widows. Zaynab died after only eight months of marriage and was buried in the Baqi' cemetery. Like Muhammad's other wives, Khadija, Sawda, Umm Salama, Rayhana, Safiyya, Hafsa, Juwayriya, Umm Habiba, and Maymuna, she too had lost her husband. Of the Prophet's wives, only 'A'isha and Zaynab b. Jahsh were exceptions to this pattern: one a virgin, the other a divorcee.

Hafsa, the Prophet's Librarian

Hafsa and 'A'isha informed their fathers about everything concerning their husband Muhammad. Having insiders in the Prophet's household, gave their fathers unique power in the *umma* and a foundation to become the first caliphs. But, despite a shared familial loyalty and strong intellects, the two wives were quite different. 'A'isha was affectionate and supportive, one of the Prophet's favorites, while Hafsa was argumentative and difficult. Her position was tenuous enough that several sources state she was divorced by Allah's Messenger and only reinstated when Gabriel urged, "O, Muhammad, take Hafsa back. She fasts and prays at night and she is one of your wives in the Garden."[121]

defiance

for Lesley H.

This poem kicks up a ruddy dust cloud,
slams doors, then holds its ground; it
leans forward, spits words, knits its brow.
You can see it chafe and grip its own hands

so the index fingers won't fly up and punch air.

This poem can amaze
with audacity, and defy Muhammad.
This poem brings him great distress.
Long ago this poem was taught to chide others;
was tongue-lashed by 'Umar from the start.

You cannot divorce this poem any more than
you can remove Hafsa from the privilege
of being the Prophet's wife in Paradise.

Despite being reinstated by Angel Gabriel, Hafsa's path was never a smooth one. She was only one of many widows of the Battle of Badr trying to find husbands. When her father, 'Umar, asked first 'Uthman, then Abu Bakr to take his daughter, each refused. In the end, it was Muhammad who remedied the difficult situation. He offered to marry the high-spirited girl, then barely nineteen. He may have had reason to regret his kindness, for his two youngest wives, Hafsa and 'A'isha, are remembered for their merriment and pranks. Frightening Sawda, just mentioned, was one. A more serious trick involved their role in preventing a marriage to Asma'. Hafsa proved to be a jealous wife and when she discovered her husband in her room with Mariya, she fumed until he promised not to spend time with the woman. If Muhammad did this to keep Hafsa from ranting to the other wives, it didn't work. Hafsa was a woman incapable of discretion. She immediately complained to 'A'isha and caused such uproar that the Prophet withdrew from all his wives for twenty-nine days and nights, as previously recounted in Mariya's story.

But Hafsa was more than just a troublemaker. She and her brother 'Abdullah, raised and educated by 'Umar, were literate. In an age when an educated woman was a rarity, the ability to read and write was prized by Muhammad, who rewarded Hafsa with his attention. One source writes: "The Holy Prophet kept her posted with the latest revelations and held frequent discourses with her on topics of [interest]. She would spend whole days attending to these talks to the exclusion of her own personal affairs."[122] After the Prophet's death during the Caliphate of Abu Bakr, the Qur'an was collected and written as one manuscript. 'Umar had six standardized copies made, and the divergent versions, burned.[123] At this time it was Hafsa who was entrusted with the original Qur'an.

Hafsa's Qur'an

Marwan, governor of Medina... sent a courier to Hafsa
asking for the folios but she refused him...
— Anas b. Malik[124].

for Hilal

Tell The Governor I say no,
I don't accept command or bribe
I do not vacillate
and you can leave, now go.

I am the Prophet's librarian. And this
is the book: al-Kitab. The only set
of Abu Bakr's folios, first copy of God's kiss.
Its ink still hums against my very skin.

The Mother Who Reads, the Prophet's librarian,
how blessed I am by al-Kitab,
which, after the last companion's gone
may wash believers in the Word-of-God

Arabic, a printed alembic architecture of light
recorded on palm stalk, on camel's
shoulder-bone, or held in memory;
copied to parchment then, and
swaddled with a length of green cloth, first

Qur'an passed from my father
down to 'Uthman, then to me. Between the leaves
is Revelation. How can someone like you understand,
Marwan? You set yourself to be the one

to grab and shred and burn
this first Qur'an (may copies rise and multiply),
as soon as I am shrouded in clean cloth
and lowered into earth.

It is unfortunate that Hafsa left no commentary on the Qur'an. She lived
those transitional moments between the oral tradition and the written. Sad-
ly, we are left with more tales of the disruption she brought to the *umma*
than lists of her contributions. This is doubtless due to the hadith's early

editors, who focused on her strong, opinionated nature to the neglect of her scholarship.

Juwayriyya, the little jewel

A dream heralded the arrival of Prophet Muhammad in Juwayriyya's life. She dreamed the moon fell in her breast. Fearful of the meaning, unlike Safiyya, she kept it a secret. When her people were defeated at the well of *al-muraysi* in 627, Barra, as she was known then, became the property of Thabit b. Qays.

As the daughter of a chief, she wasted no time in negotiating to buy her freedom as prisoners then could do. She had no trouble speaking up for herself. She demanded an audience with Muhammad.

the thirst-quenching well (*al-muraysi*)

The well would remember
that men fought over water just hours before.

The spoon would click in the cup
of the interlude, and date sugar
would sweeten the drink Muhammad sipped
at the moment she stood in his tent by the well.

It was unforgettable: her glossy words of Arabic,
his marriage offer and name change,
the catch of light on her bracelets,
and later, the ransom, the hidden camels,
the hundred freed captives.

Juwayriyya's laugh
would intoxicate the well
so it no longer remembered;
yet locals claim the water
carries traces of ambrosia.

Muhammad was taken with her. "She was a sweet woman; everyone who just saw her fell for her."[125] He offered to ransom, rename and marry her. He proposed to release the people of her tribe, the Banu al-Mustaliq, from captivity. 'A'isha said, "A hundred men, women, and children were freed on the occasion of the Prophet's marriage to Juwayriyya, and I know no woman who was more helpful to her people than she."[126]

She married Muhammad when she was twenty and lived another forty-five years. It is perplexing that her entry into the *umma* is so carefully recorded, only to render her storyless for her long life. There is something about fasting, and her death. What happened to the hadith that speak of her life as Muhammad's wife? It seems likely that her stories were weeded out, or less likely, that her influence was negligible in the family of wives.

Umm Habiba, married by a king

In the place novelists visit, that archive of characters who come to life with insistence, imagine discovering this portrait of Umm Habiba.

watching her

A loud — ha!
shows the gap in her teeth,
and a smile so big her eyes
are drawn to slits.
Here in the small room
where the women crowd,
there are stories to tell.
"You may believe this or not..."
She laughs. Her belly bounces.
She shifts the weight
of bulky breasts and hips
this Umm Habiba,
who wears soft
light cloth that covers her
like clouds over a mountain.
Her head's wrapped,
in a length of Abyssinian
textile, burnt orange and ochre
that favor her skin, and when she walks she sways,
a boat in weather.
She smells of musk and amber.
She spills out of this poem.
Tear up her picture, let no image last,
forget what she might say.
She made some jests
but no one wrote them down.

Her first name was Ramla. She took the *kunya* of her daughter, Habiba. She was from the Umayyan clan — and this last is vital to her story since the Umayya and Hashim clans continued to be enemies. Ramla married 'Ubaydullah b. Jahsh, the brother of Zaynab, the Prophet's wife, both from prominent families. It was as if these newly married children of, say, the mayor and the chief of the city council were buzzing with the words and ideas of a man their parents believed to be possessed with a demon. Like the other privileged youth they were in danger and fled into exile in Abyssinia. There was a pursuit and attempted bribe by emissaries of the families, but they were welcomed by the *Negus* and stayed for many years. She had become pregnant while in Arabia, and gave birth in that far-away capitol city of Aksum. A daughter, Habiba, was born. It was almost certainly a challenging time for her. Umm Salama and others with children who spoke her language were close by, but each woman had severed ties with her own mother, and left the family religion. As to her own faith, it can be imagined that she yearned for homeland and her teacher and the other Companions. She had given up a life of wealth and prestige for a room in a city across the sea. The words she had heard Muhammad say may have swollen in meaning and emotional weight to sustain her. Not so with her husband. As if the excitement of such a new life was not enough, 'Ubaydullah converted to Christianity and became alienated from his wife and community. Umm Habiba commented that he gave himself over to wine until he died. Then when he died, her life once again changed dramatically. According to one source, four months or so after her first husband's death in 628, when she had been in Abyssinia for twelve long years, a servant from the *Negus* came with a message; "The King says to you that the Messenger of Allah has written to him to marry you to him [Muhammad]."[127]

Umm Habiba was stunned. It was said in hadith that she gave all her jewelry to Abraha, the servant, from pure joy. Umm Habiba then chose from among the Companions in Aksum: Khalid b. Sa'id acted as her guardian in the ceremony. Ja'far and his wife Asma' and the rest of the *umma* were there to witness the proxy marriage of Umm Habiba and Muhammad, by the Abyssinian king. There were wedding gifts. Fragrance was part of the accepted conventional gifting for Muhammad, and he was strict about lavish things, so the hadith says: "The king commanded that his women send to you all the scent they have." Umm Habiba explained this gift herself: "[Abraha] brought me aloes, *wars* scent, amber and much civet (musk).

I brought all of that to the Prophet. He did not object when I wore it."[128]
Both scent and incense had great value at the time, playing a large part in
Byzantine trade with Arabia and Abyssinia. Assuming that since the *Negus*
was a head of state, and regarded Muhammad as both that and a prophet,
it would follow that the ceremony and the gifts were a bit more lavish than
what we are told.

exile

i. Foreigner in Aksum

Imagine how it chafes, the lost
Arabia, her cousin's gab gone
too, her husband's vanished touch —
gone, her favored niece, her housecats;
she misses even the desert heat.
She stands for late night prayer,
although God offers her no solace.
She kneels alone in the insect din,
the monkey screech, the hyena chuckle.
In the jungle there are more
than imaginary tigers —
how fast they take a goat, a child.

ii. *keep the faith, do good works...*
and [hold to] patience in adversity.[Q. 103: 1–3].

Here, local women have a hand-on-hip look,
visible without the hand, without the hip,
and talk a cockeyed talk she never caught
but she could understand her husband's taunts.
When *umma* families died, completely gone,
and when her angry daughter turned
her eyes away — *my mother, phagh!*
she understood a need. Then
did she set out remedies,
those tiny jars of salve and scent,
the ones to ease the rub and itch of exile?
Did she fast and keep the faith?
Did her mouth taste of Allah's word
until at last she heard Medina call?

iii. Plant a tree

After the orchids, the dress,
the wedding words, the feast, the lion on a chain,
she might appear holding the *kosso* sapling,
the tree that flowers with ten thousand stars
and sets its roots in earth. She would have helped
to dig the hole. She might say simply:
"God willing, It's my final day in Aksum.
When the end comes, plant a tree."

At this time the *Negus* was ruling a diminishing state, which was in political upheaval. The end of the empire was not long in coming and this wedding may have been one of the last happy days at the palace. Within a year, Aksum was overrun by rebels and soon the *Negus* was dead. Muhammad and the former exiled people of the *umma*, blessed by his able protection for so long, grieved for him.[129]

Her Father

But before all this could happen, sometime after 610, a clash began between the old ways, heavy with long-held proscribed and prescribed behaviors and the new ways, inspired by Muhammad's words. During this time, Abu Sufyan, the father of Ramla, as Umm Habiba was known, was a kind of "mayor" of Mecca and the quintessential old-fashioned man, while his daughter looked forward to a new order. Abu Sufyan, Umayya's grandson, had drunk from the same wet nurse as Muhammad. The milk bond meant a close family connection in Arab culture. In a dramatic twist, as the society began to shift toward the future, Abu Sufyan became the Meccan chief most actively opposed to Muhammad — in other words, his most powerful enemy. The directionality of time was viewed very differently then. From the place a man or woman stood in a caravan, behind the parents and in front of the children, the past stretched up ahead, ancestor by ancestor all the way to the first prophet, Adam. The future would continue behind, in a similar pattern, yet to be made manifest. Individual action placed one's children at risk. It looked as if Muhammad had broken the paradigm. While it seemed that he no longer followed those who had gone before him, he drew inspiration from his ancestor prophets Abraham, Moses, and Jesus — who, like himself, looked directly to God for guidance.

Abu Sufyan scolds Ramla

for Saadi

The tribe is everyone with whom you stand.
Don't switch from camel line to camel line.
Be careful not to drop your shield from hand
and tongue. Stay in your saddle, with your kind.
It's family gods and kin that count. Ignite
flame of chaos and you'll draw old ones' wrath.
Our fathers went before us, held the light
so children, coming after, see the path.
You learn, each hoof and foot inscribe the route
to ride. Forget Muhammad's charming talk.
He's Hashim. You're Umayyid. They have vowed
no friendship since the families ran amok.

Let that man go, my girl, or be forewarned.
I'll curse my fate each day — that you were born.

Clearly Ramla (Umm Habiba) and her husband ignored her father's warning and traveled to Aksum. She was followed by an envoy sent by Abu
Sufyan to bring back his daughter and the others. These were men who
tried to bribe the *Negus* — and failed. As far as Abu Sufyan was concerned,
Muhammad led a dangerous cult. He interfered as a responsible parent and
leader. Many of the Meccans felt this way.

More than a decade went by and Umm Habiba raised her daughter,
Habiba, on the African continent. Then came her estranged husband's
death and the opportunity to marry her father's nemesis. Here is the sequence: aristocratic girl and husband ran away with the followers of her
father's enemy; husband left her and the path of Islam for Christianity and
became an alcoholic; then she was married to the Prophet of Islam with
the king of Abyssinia as his proxy, and afterwards sailed east to Arabia to
be reunited with Muhammad. When Abu Sufyan heard the news, that his
enemy was his son-in-law, he must have been forced to reflect, as parents often are when children stray from their advice. Although not happy with his
daughter's choice, he resigned himself to the facts, and even acknowledged
Muhammad's ancestry and honorable behavior.

no black mark

The town seems cold beneath a slate gray sky,
all wrapped in smoke and smell of butchered meat.
That sound of goats at slaughter, how they cry!
It tries a man to pull against defeat —
bad luck, lost years, his daughter is misled.
But Sufyan shrugs and thumbs the narrow crease
along his sleeve. Because his Ramla wed
the enemy, he speaks: "To be fair, at the least,
I'll say the guy has no black mark upon
the honor vital to a man."[130] Those standing
with the elder nod and murmur in response.
One God seems like a problem that demands

so much explaining. It seems wrongheaded
to ride against a leader like Muhammad.

The verse from Revelation: *It well may be that Allah will put love between you and those of them who are your enemies.* [Q. 60:7] was a direct reference to Abu Sufyan and his daughter that brought up the issue of marriage as a link between families and tribes. The power of such a ceremony worked to bind rivals and reminded them that the well being of the group comes before that of any individual. After her marriage to Muhammad, Abu Sufyan came abruptly to his estranged daughter to ask for political aid.

Umm Habiba's room

Abu Sufyan went to see his daughter, hoping she might agree to intervene on his behalf.[131]

He never was a good listener,
doesn't wait to be asked in;
plunks himself down
on her bed, on the sheepskin,
that sweet-shop place where
her husband made a gesture
with his toothstick today, saying:
"One God! *Qul Huwal-lahu Ahad.*"

She stands, chin dropped, and stares
into the water jug she holds before her
to refresh each guest. She sweats.

Her father, Mayor of Mecca,
ally of truce-breakers has arrived.

To guide her, there are daughter's rules,
a woman's etiquette; there's adab
to hold chaos back.

His wet towel, wiped and tossed
flops on the jar rim, darkens and sinks.
She slams the whole jar down.

Get up! You can't sit here. This
is the place of Allah's Messenger.

She matches his long stare.
Hadith tells different stories here.[132]

Was there a curse? a snarl? A back-
stop phrase of poetry? Or did she

just stand there for herself,
then walk to the door
to watch him stomp away,
and say to herself, *The knife
of the family no longer cuts.*

Yet in the end, Abu Sufyan is shown to be so struck by the power and devotion of the men of the *umma*, that he said the words that joined him to
"The One God" and "Muhammad as Prophet" just before the Meccan take-
over when the idols were broken. It is probable his daughter welcomed and
received him, since he was then a Companion.

Muhammad's marriage challenges

The year 629 marked Muhammad's marriages to Umm Habiba, Safiyya,
and Maymuna, as well as the arrival of Mariya. He negotiated the peace
treaty of Hudaybiya and triumphed over Khaybar, an enemy city. This victory brought unheard-of wealth and booty for the community, his soldiers
and his followers. A life of prosperity and fame replaced that of survival;
years of semi-starvation, deprivation and want were over. The shock of
abundance created competition, dissension among the cliques of wives, the

individual wives, and between the women and their husband. In the close quarters around the first mosque in Medina lay the simple rooms housing those linked in marriage with Allah's Messenger. Each dwelling was a private room, a quiet retreat in a communal setting where a wife received her husband during her time with him. In the early years, there were two, then three or four wives, and only the barest necessities of food and shelter. But by this time the complex of rooms belonging to the wives had grown to eight or more, and comfort had come to everyone.

Now Muhammad was distracted in a new way. Mariya had arrived. Although she was a foreigner, not even an "official" wife, her presence in Muhammad's life was dazzling. He housed her some distance away from the mosque complex in upper Medina in a house with a garden. Some of the wives were envious of her and her lodgings. With prosperity, they had time for such dissatisfactions, which reached a peak in the incident of Hafsa's rage the time she discovered Allah's Messenger had entered her room with Mariya. Clearly, the situation in the harem was at a boil; prosperity, jealousy, envy and greed. Such factors could upset two married people, then add eight or so wives, with whom there were delicate diplomatic ties, reaching deep into the web of alliances. The unrest even caused comment in the wider sphere: 'Umar said to his daughter Hafsa, "O, my little daughter, are you [really] talking back to the Messenger of God up to the point that he remains angry the whole day?" Hafsa said, "By God we do talk back to him."[133]

It was this tumult Muhammad withdrew from to reflect on a course of action. During the month he was gone, the women were uneasy and fearful; no one knew if his retreat was temporary or would lead to wholesale divorce.

on the porch

Muhammad climbs to the porch and pulls the ladder up.
He carries his gear,   water skin, blanket, tooth stick.
Below, where the women chatter,   relentless as cicadas,

caught in faction and backtalk, chit-chat and story
telling,   the place is struck with unnatural quiet.
When will he come down?   The wives are waiting.

The first night, when he would have slept with her,
Umm Salama sits in the dark, combs out her thick braid

with lote-tree oil and gathers the hairs from the comb one by one.
Juwayriyya's night, she fasts and dreams a feast,
blinks awake to the scratch of mattress twigs,   rubs at
the saliva mark on her pillow. By the third night,

Umm Habiba is repeating God's name,
when Mu'ayza, Muhammad's cat, climbs in her lap
and begins purring. When she drifts off, the cat nudges her awake.

The fourth night, Hafsa's night, she cries in her room.
Her harsh father shouts at her through the window,
Serves you right if he jilts you.

On her night, Zaynab tends a sick bird squeezing
drops of water into the open beak from her knotted handkerchief.
All night she shelters the bird between her breasts.

Nearly every night, 'A'isha runs out to the lava field. She hurries
through the reek of goats, her shawl flapping.
When she reaches the well edge, she leans over, screams

into stone darkness with the lost voice of Sarah, of Hagar, of Mariam,
with the pain of all the women who love the one
whose tongue and heart belong to God. On the twenty-ninth day,

Muhammad comes down from the porch.

At the end of the month, 'Umar, gravely concerned, went to check on the
Prophet and asked if he meant to divorce his wives. Muhammad answered
with a smile and 'Umar understood and shouted loudly, Praise God! (*al-
hamdul'illah*) so everyone knew that a higher message had come through:
[Q. 33:28, 29, 32].

> O Prophet, Say to your wives: "In case you desire the life and pomp of this
> world, come, I will provide you handsomely, and let you go with a grace.
> But if you desire God, His Apostle and the joys of life to come, then God
> has verily set apart for those of you who do good works, a great reward...O
> wives of the Prophet, you are not like other women.

As powerful as this message seems in English, it pales in comparison to the
Arabic; the layered meanings and the rich tapestry of allusion and nuance
are lost. But we must try to imagine how dynamic the impact was on the

women sharing a life with Muhammad. It was Allah's direct request for each of them to make a deeper commitment and the concurrent promise of direct support from Allah. This was more than a husband asking a wife to try harder to be a worthy partner. Each wife was asked to align her life's purpose with that of Muhammad, and to surrender her ego directly to the One God. From the point of view of the mystic, they were to dedicate their lives to love for and in service of the Divine Reality. Since the wives had also been through thirty days of internal dialog, of prayer and introspection, they may have asked questions such as: What could it mean, "Only Allah?" Where was the real value in life? How did a woman set an example for those who looked up to her?

Without scolding or criticism, Muhammad restored harmony. Every wife pledged to accept the new level of commitment. Now the wives were becoming more focused on the path of peaceful self-surrender to the same Source. Perhaps there is no place in the hadith or the Qur'an where these women were suddenly described as *Mothers of the Faithful*, but this moment they were raised to a place of greater respect. The Companions recognized this greater dignity as well. It must have brought the wives together more than any one thing except Muhammad's death.

Asma', the unfortunate one

There are women who were almost married to Muhammad, married briefly, or divorced right away. Asma' b. an-Nu'man, a young widow, was among them. It was this wife Asma', whose marriage to Muhammad was destroyed by the meddling of the wives, 'A'isha and Hafsa, and devious mischief.

There was reason for the wives' discomfort with Asma'. Hadith describes her as "the most beautiful and youthful of her people." Another source writes: "She was the most beautiful of all women and the Prophet's wives were afraid she would gain precedence with him over them..."[134] The wives were put off because they saw her as a foreigner, as she came from an area east of Medina, a place that had different customs than theirs. But it was precisely this foreignness that interested Muhammad. He was making an alliance with her tribe. In 631 her father drew up the marriage contract, and she came to the home of a family in the *umma*. This would have made her the last wife, since he died the next year.

At first 'A'isha and Hafsa appeared to welcome Asma' when she arrived as a bride. They hennaed her hands and feet and combed her hair, pretending to give her love advice, while teaching her the words for the divorce formula. They dared to persuade her that repeating those words would make the Prophet love her more. He, of course, heard the formula as a powerful repudiation, and sent her home, although she protested that she had been tricked. She was from that time on considered married, and so bound not to marry another man. She may have remarried, although one source claims: "No one sought to marry her and she was not seen by anyone except relatives until her death…she died disconsolate."[135]

Mrs. Muhammad

This is for you, girl —
sent home to the Najd with two white dresses;
when the month of June was over.
You, the pretty one who calls herself *the wretch*.

This is for the girl — that's you,
who never got to touch
her husband's hand
or even be kissed by him.

This is for you, girl —
the fool in a word trap. Trapped.
On your wedding day
you repeat the phrase
his youngest wife, 'A'isha, said
would make him love you
more. But look, his arm flies up
to hide his face,
and then he's gone.

This is for you, Asma' b. al-Nu'man b. Abil-Jawn
Mrs. Muhammad until you die.
The fall
is lifelong, to the knees.[136]

This is a tragic story of beauty and misfortune that demonstrates only too clearly the power of ritual and custom and of rites so strange to a foreign bride, that she could be caught by its ambiguity, a foolish, unsuspecting girl. Such naïveté could put the *umma* at risk. There were other women who almost married Muhammad. Illness, disapproval or bad timing may have contributed to these failed alliances. Asma' holds the place in this story for these women who, due to misfortune, stopped a phrase or two away from being married to Muhammad.

Maymuna, the last Wife

Martin Lings describes how Muhammad rode his white camel, Qaswa, into the empty city of Mecca in 629. The Meccan chiefs, gathered on hill nearby, watched the long dust cloud rise as two thousand pilgrims, dressed in white, walked single file behind him. Muhammad had negotiated this alternative pilgrimage (*'umra*), or three-day sacred visit to the Ka'ba as part of the Peace Treaty at Hudaybiya the year before. When the two groups were in proximity, members of both sides held joyful reunions with estranged family and friends. Such was the case with Muhammad's youngest uncle, 'Abbas, who offered Maymuna (his widowed sister-in-law) to him in marriage.

As a boy, Muhammad was nurtured by his grandfather in Mecca; this marriage to Maymua rejoined him to his father's family. Muhammad agreed and wanted to have a celebration immediately, inside Mecca. But local leaders objected, and escorted the pilgrims out of the city on the third day, as planned. Muhammad stopped at a nearby town called Sarif, married her, and sacrificed an oxen for the marriage celebration. This tied Mecca with Medina, bringing close connections into the *umma*.

These alliances included the champion warrior of the time, a man named Khalid, Maymuna's nephew. Maymuna's birth name was Barra (as was Juwayriyya). Allah's Messenger gave her the name Maymuna, which means "blessed." She was about 30 years old when they married on the seventh of February, 629. She died in 681 and was buried in Sarif, according to Al-Tabari; this makes her the last wife married, and the last to die.

Maymuna and Muhammad

The first taste was a roan-
red date she placed
between his lips.
He spoke in *nuquul* to her:
mmm and aaah,
called her *Maymuna,*

no longer, "the dutiful one." *Maii…*,
a breeze in fronds; its frictions
polishing green nubs to fruit.
The flavor of the name was good.
She savored the vowels,
sent Mm's and Nnn down
to hold the hem of her faith
like palm roots in oasis soil.

He severed the Bah's and Raws
of her former name, urged a boy up a tree
with a knife in his teeth
to cut a spathe laden with crown jewels,
his dower gift —
eighty measures of *Deglet Noor*.

The first taste she gave him was
the completed date: *tamr* —
perfect, self-preserving, succulent.
Maymuna, his last wife, conversed
in "pieces of light" bit into the language
which sustained them all;
'Anbara, from one oasis;
Safwi, Sukkari, from another.

The final taste she gave him
was a sip of cool date broth, when
he collapsed. That night
wind ravaged the palmary. Stars tossed
in the unquiet sky. The morning ground
was littered with oval fruit
fallen too soon. [137]

In the year 630, at the conquest of Mecca, Maymuna was waiting at the Prophet's red leather tent with Fatima and Umm Salama. They greeted him, and helped him with his ablutions and the transition from leader of the army to Allah's Messenger with the daunting task of altering the belief system of Mecca forever. They watched as he mounted Qaswa, said the sacred phrase, and broke the idols.

It was on Maymuna's "day" that Muhammad began suffering from his final illness, in the year 632, just two years after he claimed Mecca in the name of Islam (which means "peaceful surrender"). She lived to be eighty or eighty-one, and is described as a strong woman.

⚜ ⚜

A picture of the beginnings of Islam can be seen through the frame of Muhammad's respect for women and the influence upon him of matriarchal tradition. He treated marriage as a partnership, begun with the consent of both parties. He must have felt responsibility for women around him who lacked a protector; he behaved with tenderness toward those in his care. While Allah's Messenger might have cemented alliances with groups and individuals through marriage, he also listened to his wives and daughters. The hadith about these women of the *umma*, illuminate a path through the dense patriarchy that exists around the family of the Prophet.

Muhammad's wives, later his widows, were brave and bold enough to lead the way to a larger life, especially into the unknown landscape of the new Islamic impulse — not even a religion yet. As a social institution, marriage can be seen as impacting kin, clan and the collective future of a people. However, it is clear in these pages that most every woman married to Muhammad held some traits of desire, aversion, jealousy and pride, and those very challenges may have helped her to polish her inner jewel and that of her husband. The distinguished Professor Emeritus Huston Smith once told me (regarding his wife, Kendra), "My partner and I have been honing each other's rough edges for sixty years. And I still have rough edges!" Muhammad is known as "the Complete Man," yet how do we conceive such a lofty Ideal? Over the years he ripened into a partner of deep understanding as well as a very human husband. In this, he serves as an example to countless Muslims and to humanity.

In conclusion: those who study the Mothers of Islam can take comfort in the fact that each wife had her own personal frailties, which may be just as vital as her better-known stories of generosity, insight, and deep commitment. We honor each woman for a life well lived, but we also need to be careful not to idealize her, for by doing so, we remove her individual strength and uniqueness. Muhammad once said that Paradise lies beneath the feet of the mothers. To honor them, we need to hold both his words and their everyday reality in a continual balance.

Wife of the Prophet

It is the way for the Wife of the Prophet
not to turn her back on us. After
she notices we are looking to her, she opens the door
and beckons us in. But we are just watchers,
wanting to be close-up from a distance. We stare
at one young wife, leaning forward, her chin
on Muhammad's shoulder, her fingers
squeezing his arm while the Abyssinian woman
dances. Another wife gives Muhammad
a turn of phrase to calm a thousand
disobedient men. We notice the well-shaped
mouth, the strong white teeth,
her damp hands on a towel. A future wife
stands looking at Muhammad's open face.
We hear her gasp and understand. She's modest. Still,
we can't stop looking. Close details
make each wife's bustling seem intimate,
but not too real. We wonder what we'd see
inside. There might be holy striving,
talk of paradise, a questioning remark,
a judgment. We may never know,
although there may be truth there
that we need, some understanding
from the source; some word of how it was
before something startled the world
into thinking — us and them.[138]

THE CLOSING POEM

how the story goes

for Ahamed Muhaiyaddeen

❊❊ ❊❊

Eve

The Arabs have a version from Qur'an.
Forget what you have learned about the apple.
I'm a woman come to them
without a snake, or craft or blame.

Grandmother Eve, the Wife
of Prophet Adam: I am
the first! We fell of course.
We were forgetful, ate,
and left that heavenly light too soon.
We disobeyed—and Allah forgave us.[139]

My grave lies east of the Red Sea
drawing the generations—
children, children's children, all posterity
to that once sacred place, paved over
where the concrete desecrates
the earth our bones have blessed!

In Mecca, where Khadija rests,
her plot was spoiled; and here's
Medina's cemetery bulldozed flat.
'A'isha and the others lie beneath
an empty field of dust. [140]

No cherished markers over
honored bones, those gravestones stripped
by jittery men who forgot what Muhammad said,
ignored his words:

Paradise lies at the feet of the Mothers[141].

show us

We all rest then travel, travel then sleep,
and wake to follow Grandmother Eve,
the other wives, the orange moon, the fragrance
of Damascus Rose, smoked resin,
sweat and camel dung, the quiet that
surrounds the final hour's ride.

The girl working the ropes
of an agitated mule frees the load
without getting kicked. The knots are tight.
There's the snake, the clutched leaves,
the nakedness that never ends.
Paradise lies at the feet of the mothers.
The ropes ease and the mule settles down.
In Eve's story the trail of her camel
is the path, the way of a seeker,
the *din* to return to Allah.[142]

Look down from your walking camels,
Mothers, bless me, call out last words
as you depart and I stand here
about to close the book

and pass into this time's top-heavy world—
that, if it were a howdah,
could pull a camel down and spill us out.

Remind me here,
so I will never forget:
neither war, nor words
will give us ease.
Tell me again how best
to honor that Paradise and show
me and others
the Garden's path (*the mustaqim*)
is mercy, compassion, and a gentle breath.

dedication

What is written for us, by us, in us
is the signature of what we love,
set down in the bright language of the heart.
Let it be known!

Glossary

abu. Father of —

adab. Important principle in the Muslim world, refined behavior, politeness; and doing the right thing at the right time for the right reason: kind, and chivalrous action

Abyssinia. A Christian kingdom (once a vast empire) including Ethiopia, Eritrea, and Sudan where Muhammad sent some of his early followers for protection

Adulis. The main port for the Abyssinian Empire in present day Eritrea

Aksum. Capital of The Abyssinian Empire in present day Ethiopia

Ahl al-bayt. The descendants of the Prophet, from Fatima and 'Ali

al-batin, al-zahir. The inner and the outer (attributes of Allah)

al-hamdu'lillah. Praise God

al-ilah. (The god), the creator god of pre-Islam, the one behind all the deities

al-Kitab. The Book, refers to the Qur'an

Allahu akbar. God is the greatest

al-rahman, al-rahim. Names of God, meaning the Merciful and the Compassionate. Also written as ar-Rahman ar-Rahim

Ansar. The helpers from Medina who hosted the Muslim refugees from Mecca

'aziz. (ya 'aziz). God's aspect of strength, power, preciousness and nobility

'Attar. Fariduddin 'Attar, (12th c.). Persian poet who wrote *The Conference of the Birds*

b. (bana). Abbreviation of Ibn, the son of —

b. (bint). Daughter of —

Baqi' cemetery. Place where most of Muhammad's wives and children were buried

Battle of the Camel. First civil war within the Islamic community in 656

bay'at. An oath of allegiance as in *bay'at al-ridwan*. Later came to have the meaning of "initiation"

bet midrash. (Hebrew) House of study

caliph. Political leader of the Muslim community, literally meaning successor of Muhammad

caliphate. The political office of leader of the Muslim community after Muhammad's death

Companions (*al-sahaba*). Anyone who met Muhammad in person, generally the first generation of Muslims

Coptic. The language of Egypt after Christianization (now only a liturgical language), also referring to the distinctly Egyptian denomination of Christianity, i.e., the "Coptic Church"

dajjal. Antichrist

dhikr. Remembrance, repeating the name(s) of God [see zikr]

dibaja. Brocade, introductory verses, style, elegance, prestige

din. Religion, in a mystical sense: "the path of return to Allah."

djelaba. Outer garment (robe) worn in Morocco

fajr. Dawn — usually used to denote the dawn prayer

falatya. Inappropriate, wanton behavior

Fatiha. The opening sura of the Qur'an, recited many times in ritual prayer

fitna. Chaos, disorder

hadith. Transmissions, now written and canonized, of what Muhammad said and did

hakim. Literally a wise person, sometimes used for judge and in the Indian Subcontinent; a practitioner of Greek medicine

hilm. Gentleness, patience, discernment. From the root *Halama*: to dream or meditate on, also the attribute of God: *Ya-Halim*, meaning, Oh Gentle, Mild, and Kind One

hanif. Early monotheists, followers of Abrahamic tradition at the time of the Prophet

Haw'ab. A town near Basra, where the "dogs barked"

hijab. Curtain, veil

Hijaz. The area of Northwestern Arabia including Mecca and Medina, bordering on the Red Sea

hijra. Migration; refers to the migration to Medina in the year 622 CE, which is year one, in the Islamic calendar

howdah. Enclosed platform set on a large animal (camel) to ride on

hu. Essence of the Essence, esoteric sound of Allah (the last syllable of *Al-lahu*)

Hudaybiya. Place near Mecca where Muhammad brought about a peace treaty in 628

'id or Eid. Typically there are two Eids in the Islamic calendar celebrating the end of Ramadan and the completion of the hajj

isnad. Chain of transmitters that has to be authentic for a hadith to be sound *islam.* From the root s-l-m meaning, among other things safety, surrender, peace. Came to have a technical meaning after the Prophet: Surrender to God, which became reified as *Islam* as a name of a religion

jahiliyya. Era before Islam, with fierce barbaric attitudes; known as the era of ignorance

jihad. Struggle or striving

jihad **of restraint.** Discretionary advice for women of the Prophet

greater *jihad.* The struggle with one's nafs or ego

lesser *jihad.* Physically struggling typically in battle or war

Ka'ba. Ancient sanctuary at Mecca, which is the direction toward which Muslims pray

kalb. Dog

kasara. To break, break open

kashaf. Unveil, uncover

Khaybar. Wealthy oasis city conquered by Muhammad, where Safiyya lived

kitab. The (a) book, any book (Refers here to the Qur'an)

kohl. Black eye-liner with beauty-enhancing as well as medicinal properties

Koran. Alternative spelling of the word Qur'an

kunta ajidu. From *wajada* (to be in a painful state of agitation)

kunya. Honorific, including the placing of *Umm* (mother of) or *Abu* (father of) before one's name

la ilaha illa 'llah. There is no God; this phrase often used for Rememberance"

majdhub. One who is "crazy" with God-intoxication

maghrib. Sunset typically used to denote the Sunset prayer

manna gum. Foul-smelling plant substance

maqam. Station, spiritual placement, degree of internal refinement

Mawlud. Celebration of the birth of Prophet Muhammad (yearly)

Medina. The city known as Yathrib where Muhammad migrated with his people in 622

midrash **(Hebrew).** Debate to clarify commentary on religious questions

Mother of the Faithful. Name for Prophet Muhammad's wives and daughters

muqarabun. From *qarib*, close or near, refers to the "People of the Bench," sincere practitioners, near the Prophet's mosque. Also known as *Ahl al-suffa*

Mu'ayza. The name of Muhammad's cat, means "little sweetie"

Muharram. First month of the Islamic calendar

mu'min. One who stays true to a trust, a "believer"

munaffiqun. Hypocrites

Muqawqis. Archbishop of Egypt at the time of Muhammad

mustaqim. The straight path (to Allah)

nabi. A prophet

nafas. Breath

nafs. Soul, ego-self depending on the context

People of the Bench. *ahl al-suffa*, meaning bench or porch called the *muqarabun* (from *qarib*, the root is *qaraba* translated, "one who comes close or near" (to Allah)

People of the Book. Jews, Christians, Sabians, and Muslims: those with a revealed book

Pir. Persian term for leader of a sufi lineage, a spiritual mentor. Lit. old

Phlox Maculata. A cool weather shade plant with lovely flowers. Phlox (Gr.) means "flame."

polytheism. Belief and worship of multiple deities

prosimetrum. (Latin), narrative with poetry embedded in it; the format of this book

qalb. Heart

qari'a. "Calamity," also the name of Sura 101 (Qur'an)

Qaswa. Endurance, also the name of Muhammad's she-camel

Qur'an. Lit.: recitation. The primary scripture for Muslims revealed by God to Muhammad (sometimes spelled Koran)

Rabb. Refers to God; Sustainer, Cherisher, Lord

Ramadan. Month of fasting in the Islamic calendar

rasul. *Rasulullah,* Messenger of God (Muhammad's title)

ridwan. "Good pleasure," refers to affirming an agreement with Muhammad at Hudaybiya. See *bay'a*

sadaqa. Charitable giving

Sakina (Ar), **Shekina** (Hebrew). She-Who-is-God's Presence

as-salamu 'aluykum. May peace be upon you.

salat. Ritual prayer performed five times daily

samun. Hot, intense sandstorm

shahid. (root: *shahada*) means witness with a long vowel a and martyrdom with a long vowel i

Second Temple. The reconstructed temple in Jerusalem 518 BCE to 70 CE, destroyed by the Romans (The First Temple was known as Solomon's Temple)

Shi'a. Those who think that 'Ali should have been Muhammad's successor. Now roughly 15% of the Muslim population, mostly in Iran with different variations on ritual practices from the Sunnis

Shi'atu 'Ali. The Party of 'Ali

shirk. Ascribing partners to God; (as in Father, Son and Holy Ghost), considered blasphemy by Muslims

Shu'ayba. The Arabian port on the Red Sea; departure point for Abyssinia

subhan Allah. Glory to God!

sufi. Mystical tradition with ancient origins; Lit. a person who wears wool; A person who does more than the Islamic ritual requirements in order to have an experience of God in this life

Sufi Ruhaniat International, Sufi Order International, International Sufi Movement, Sufi Way. All are sufi groups affiliated with the teachings of Hazrat Inayat Khan in the Chishti Lineage that was founded by the Indian sufi, Mu'inuddin Chishti (d. 1236)

sunna. What the Prophet Muhammad used to do

Sunni. The majority group who agree that Abu Bakr was the rightful successor to Muhammad and who ruled the Islamic world for many centuries

sura. A chapter in the Qur'an; There are 114 suras in the Qur'an

tasbih. Rosary, prayer beads

Thout, Kioahk, Tobe, Paremonde, Pachons, and Mesore. Coptic names of the months

umma. Name given to the Muslim community

Umm. Mother of —

ummahat al-mu'minin. Mothers of Islam (lit.), refers to Muhammad's wives

'umra. The "lesser pilgrimage to Mecca, not made during the yearly *hajj* time

wadhifas **(wazifas).** The ninety-nine names of Allah, given in Sufism as practice; each a formula to transform a condition (example: *al-sabur*, patience) recognizable in this text as attributes (Compassionate, Noble) that begin with a capital letter

Wahhabi. Puritanical sect of Islam founded by Muhammad Ibn 'Abdul Wahhab in the eighteenth century and who helped the House of Sa'ud come to power

wars. The word *wars* may have been confused with *ward* (rose blossoms).

Yahudiyya. Jewish dialect related to Hebrew, used in seventh c. Arabia

Yathrib. The name of the city of Medina before Muhammad's arrival

Zamzam. The well found by Hagar in Mecca when she was left by Prophet Abraham and rediscovered by Muhammad's grandfather, 'Abd al-Muttalib

zikr **or** *dhikr.* Remembrance (lit.), Sufi chanting or repetition of litanies

Zoroastrian. An Iranian religion founded by Zoroaster.

Muhammad's wives and the year of marriage

Khadija   594–619*

Sawda   620

'A'isha   624

Hafsa   625

Zaynab b. Khuzayma   625–626*

Umm Salama   626

Zaynab b. Jahsh   627

Juwayriyya   627

Rayhana   628–630* (not usually listed as a wife)

Umm Habiba   629

Safiyya   629

Mariya   629 (not usually listed as a wife)

Maymuna   629

Asma'   631 (immediately divorced)

* died while Muhammad was living

Muhammad died in 632, leaving 9 wives, 10 including Mariya.

Index of Names

'Abdullah b. 'Abd al-Muttalib. Muhammad's father who died before his son was born

'Abdullah b. al-Asad, Abu Salama. Husband of Hind (Umm Salama)

'Abbas b. 'Abd al-Muttalib. Muhammad's uncle

'Abd al-Muttalib. Muhammad's powerful grandfather

Abraham. Prophet and ancestor of Jews, Christians and Muslims

Abu'l-'As the son of Rabi'. Muhammad and Khadija's son-in-law; Zaynab's husband

Abu Bakr. Muhammad's close friend, father of 'A'isha, and first caliph

Abu Jahl. Meccan, nicknamed "father of Jahiliyya" by the Companions he tormented

Abu Salama ('Abdullah). Husband of Umm Salama (Hind)

Abu Sufyan b. Harb. Father of Umm Habiba. Meccan chief who fought against Muhammad

Abu Talib b. 'Abd al-Muttalib. Muhammad's uncle, guardian, and protector

Al-'Alawi, Ahmad. Sufi Master from Algeria, 1869-1934; founder of the 'Alawiyya sufis

Allat. One of the three mediating deities (goddesses) in the Arabian Peninsula before Islam

'Ali. Cousin of Muhammad who was raised in Khadija's household and married Fatima

al-'Uzza. One of the three deity mediators (goddesses) in the Arabian Peninsula before Islam

Amina b. Wahb. Muhammad's mother who died when he was seven

Ar-Rasul. *Rasulullah,* Messenger of God (Muhammad's title)

Anas b. Malik. Muhammad's friend; present when the hijab verses were spoken

Asma' b. al-Nu'man. Married to Muhammad, but tricked into instant divorce

Asma' b. Umays. Wife of Ja'far, and Abu Bakr

Barra. Juwayriyya and Maymuna's name before Muhammad changed it

Eve. Wife of Prophet Adam, expelled from the Garden and forgiven by Allah

Fatima b. Muhammad. Khadija and Muhammad's fourth daughter; 'Ali's wife

Gabriel. The angel of revelation to Muhammad and Mary, Mother of Jesus

Habiba. The daughter of Umm Habiba and 'Ubaydullah, born in Abyssinia

Hafsa b. 'Umar. Muhammad's wife and 'Umar's daughter

Hagar. Sara's handmaiden, mother of Ishmael, direct ancestor of the Muslims

Hanif. Believer in One God, before and during the time of Muhammad

Hasan b. Thabit. Poet, Companion; spread scandal or support

Hasan b. 'Ali. Muhammad and Khadija's eldest grandson by Fatima

Hashim. The Meccan clan Muhammad belonged to. Rivals with Umayyah

Hatib b. Abi Balta'a. The diplomat who brought Mariya from Egypt

Hazrat Inayat Khan. Indian sufi and musician who came to the West in 1910

Hind b. 'Utbah (Umm Salama). Prophet's wife after 'Abdullah, (Abu Salama) died

Humaira. Nick-name Muhammad gave 'A'isha, "little reddish one"

Husayn b. 'Ali. Muhammad and Khadija's second grandson by Fatima

Ibrahim b. Muhammad. Muhammad's son by Mariya who died before the age of two

Ja'far b. Abi Talib. Muhammad's cousin and Muslim leader in Abyssinia

Juwayriyya b. al-Harith. Married to Muhammad after being a captive, freed her people

Khadija b. Khuwaylid. Muhammad's only wife for twenty-five years

Manat. One of the three deities (goddesses) in the Arabian Peninsula before Islam

Mariya. Egyptian Copt, Mother of Muhammad's son, Ibrahim; probable wife to Muhammad

Maymuna b. al-Harith. Sister of Uncle 'Abbas who was married to Muhammad

Mu'awiya. The first Umayyad caliph after 'Ali's death

Mu'ayza. Muhammad's cat, translation: "little sweetie"

Mughiana, (Morgiana). Name of heroine in 'Ali Baba." From Arabic root: gh-n-y meaning free from want

Muqawqis. Title of Bishop or ruler in Egypt who sent Mariya to Muhammad

Murshid Samuel Lewis. Sufi master from San Francisco, California, 1896-1971

Negus (Nejashi). Christian emperor of Abyssinia, (Ethiopia)

Qaswa. Muhammad's camel at the Peace treaty of Hudaybiya

Quraysh. Ruling tribe of Mecca who opposed Islam; also Muhammad's tribe

Qurayzah. Jewish tribe that betrayed Muhammad; Rayhana's people

Ramla. Umm Habiba's name before she became mother of Habiba

Ruqayya b. Muhammad. Khadija and Muhammad's second daughter

Safiyya b. Bashshama. She chose captivity over marriage to Muhammad

Safiyya b. Huyay. Muhammad's second Jewish wife

Sarah. Prophet Abraham's wife who sent Hagar away to Mecca

Sawda b. Zam'a. Second wife of Muhammad

Shaharazad. Shaharazad has many spellings. The Persian is *shahrizad*, meaning "city-born princess" or "one of high birth."

Shekina (Hebrew), Sakina (Arabic). Tranquility, peace

Shirin. Mariya's sister who came with her from Egypt

Ubaydullah b. Jahsh. Zaynab's brother, Umm Habiba's first husband

'Umar b. Khattab. Close friend of Muhammad; Hafsa's father and second caliph.

Umayyah. A Meccan clan in opposition to the clan of Hashim (Muhammad's clan) after Mu'awiya seized the caliphate

Umm Abi-ha. "The Mother of her Father" name for Fatima, the Prophet's daughter

Umm Ayman. Servant of Prophet's mother, Amina; became a Companion and lived a long life

Umm Habiba (Ramla). Daughter of Abu Sufyan, married to Muhammad

Umm Kulthum b. Muhammad. Khadija and Muhammad's third daughter

Umm Salama (Hind b. Abi Umayyah). Married to Muhammad

'Uthman b. 'Affan. Muhammad's close friend, son-in-law twice, and caliph

Waraqah b. Nawfal. Khadija's uncle, a *hanif*, (believer in One God)

Zayd b. al-Harith. Muhammad's adopted son; once married to Zaynab

Zaynab b. Jahsh. Married Muhammad after being divorced from Zayd

Zaynab b. Khuzayma. Married to Muhammad for only eight months

Zaynab b. Muhammad. Eldest daughter of Khadija and Muhammad

Zaynab b. 'Ali. Surviving daughter of Fatima and 'Ali

Works Consulted

Books

Abbott, Nabia, *Aishah, the Beloved of Mohammed*, London, Saqi Books, 1998.

Anon., *The Arabian nights*, New York, Dodd, Mead, and Company, 1917.

Armstrong, Karen, *Muhammad, A Biography of the Prophet*, New York, Harper, San Francisco, 1992.

— *Muhammad, A Prophet for Our Time*, New York, Harper One, 2006.

Aslan, Reza, *No god but God*, New York, Random House, 2005.

Barlas, Asma', *"Believing Women" in Islam; Unreading Patriarchal Interpretations of the Qur'an*, Austin, University of Texas Press, 2002.

Farooqi, M.I.H., *Plants of the Qur'an*, Lucknow, Sidrah Pub., 2000.

Goehring, James, *Ascetics, Society, and the Desert: Studies in Egyptian Monasticism* (Harrisburg, PA: Trinity, 1999).

Goldzhier, Ignaz, *Muslim Studies,* 2 vols. trans. by C.R. Barber and S.M. Stern, Chicago: Aldine Inc., 1971.

Griggs, C. Wilfred, *Early Egyptian Christianity: From Its Origins to 451*, C.E. Leiden: E.J. Brill, 1990.

Helminski, Camille Adams, Women of Sufism, A Hidden Treasure, Shambhala, Boston, 2003.

Ibn al-Arabi, *Ahkam al-Qur'an*, vol. 3. ed. Abdul-Qader Atta, Beirut, Dar al-Kutub al-Ilmiyah, Pub., 1988.

Ibn Ishaq, *The Life of Muhammad*, trans. by A. Guillaume, New York, Oxford University Press, 2003.

Ibn Kathir, *The Life of the Prophet Muhammad,* trans. by, Trevor Le Gassick, Vol. IV, Reading, UK, Garnet Pub., 2000.

Ibn Sa'd, *The Women of Madina, al-Kitab at-Tabaqat al-Kabir*, vol. VIII, trans. by Aisha Bewley, London, Ta-Ha Pub., 1997.

Joannes, Bishop of Nikiou, *The Chronicle of John, Bishop of Nikiu*, trans., from Zotenberg's Ethiopic Text by R.H. Charles, London, Williams and Northgate, 1916.

Khalid, Abd'l Karim, *Ibrahim, Son of the Prophet*, Chicago, The Open School, 1996.

Khan, Hazrat Inayat, *The Heart of Sufism*, Boston, Shambhala, 1999.

Khan, Hazrat Inayat, *The Sufi Message of Hazrat Inayat Khan*, vol. IX: *The Unity of Religious Ideals* (London: Camelot Press, 1963)

Lings, Martin, *Muhammad*, New York, Inner Traditions International, 1983.

— *A Sufi Saint in the Twentieth Century*, Berkeley, University of California Press, 1973.

MacCoul, Leslie, *Coptic Perspectives on Late Antiquity*, Brookfield, Variorum, 1993.

Madelung, Wilferd, *The Succession to Muhammad*, Cambridge, Cambridge University Press, 1997.

Malik, Fida Hussain, *Wives of the Holy Prophet*, Delhi, Taj Pub. 1997.

Marlowe, John, *The Golden Age of Alexandria*, London, Victor Gollancz Ltd., 1971.

Mena of Nikiou, *The Life of Isaac of Alexandria*, trans. by David N. Bell, Kalamazoo, Cistercian Pub., 1988.

Munro-Hay, Stuart, *Aksum, An African Civilization of Late Antiquity*, Edinburgh, Edinburgh University Press,1991.

Newby, Gordon Darnell, *A History of the Jews of Arabia*, University of South Carolina Press, 1988.

Pearson, Birger, *Gnosticism, Judaism, and Egyptian Christianity*, Minneapolis: Fortress, 1990.

Pearson, Birger and James Goehring, eds., *The Roots of Egyptian Christianity*, Philadelphia: Fortress, 1986.

Peters, F.E., *Muhammad and the Origins of Islam*, Albany, State University of New York Press, 1994.

Qureshi, Sultan Ahmed, trans. *Letters of The Holy Prophet*, Karachi, International Islamic Publishers, 1983.

Roded, Ruth, *Woman in Islamic Biographical Collections*, Boulder, Lynne Rienner Pub., Boulder, 1994.

Rogers, Clive, ed., *Early Islamic Textiles*, Brighton, UK. Rogers & Podmore, 1983.

Schimmel, Annemarie, *And Muhammad Is His Messenger*, Chapel Hill, University of North Carolina Press, 1985.

Schoff, Wilfred H., *Periplus of the Erythraen Sea* (First c. Graeco-Egyptian trading manual). New Delhi, Munshiram Pub., 2001.

Spellberg, D.A., *Politics, Gender and the Islamic Past, the legacy of 'A'isha B. Abi Bakr*, New York, Columbia University Press, 1994.

Stowasser, Barbara Freyer, *Women in the Qur'an, Traditions, and Interpretation*, New York, Oxford University Press, 1994.

al-Tabari, Abu Ja'far Muhammad, *The History of al-Tabari*, vol.VI, "Muhammad at Mecca," trans. by W. Montgomery Watt and M.V. McDonald, New York, SUNY Press, 1988.

—*The History of al-Tabari*, vol.VIII, "The Victory of Islam, Muhammad at Medina," trans., Michael Fishbein, New York, SUNY Press, 1997.

— *The History of al-Tabari*, vol.IX, "The Last Years of the Prophet," trans. by, Ishmael K. Poonawala, New York, SUNY Press, 1990.

— *The History of al-Tabari*, vol.XXXIX. "Biographies of the Prophet's Companions and their Successors," trans. by, Ella Landau Tasseron, New York, SUNY Press, 1998.

— *Jami' al-bayan fi tafsir al-Qur'an*, 30 vols. Beirut: Dar al-Ma'rifa, 1980 (in Arabic).

Watt, W. Montgomery, *Muhammad at Medina*, London, Oxford University Press, 1962.

The Qur'ans and the Bible

Alim (Islamic software). *CD-ROM*, Release 6.0. Silver Spring Md., ISL Software Corp., 2000.

Qur'an, trans. by 'Ali, Ahmed, Princeton, Princeton University Press, 1993.

The Message of the Qur'an, trans. by, Muhammad Asad, Bristol, The Book Foundation, 2003.

The Holy Bible, American Bible Society, Nelson and Sons, N.Y. 1901.

Thesis, Articles, Lectures, Journalism

Ahmed, Irfan, "The Destruction of the Holy Sites in Mecca and Medina," and "The House of Sayyida Khadija in Mecca," *Islamica Magazine*, Issue 15, 2006.

Akram, Dr. Muhammad, Research Fellow at Oxford Center for Islamic Studies, "A glimpse at Early Women Islamic Scholars," from a lecture delivered September 2007.

al-Gharbi, Iqbal, "Memoires Feminines: Femmes et Politique en Islam," *Middle East Transparent*, October 18, 2004.

Kern, Linda Lee, *The Riddle of 'Umar al-Khattab, in Bukhari's Kitab al-Jami' as Sahih*, Ph.D. thesis, Harvard University, June, 1996.

Online News Hour with Jim Lehrer, 2/19/02: by correspondent Elizabeth Farnsworth from an interview: Dr. Sami Angawi, (Saudi Architect from an old Jeddah family descended from the Prophet).

Select Dictionaries and Encyclopedias

Encyclopedia Coptica, The Christian Coptic Orthodox Church of Egypt, <u>www. coptic.net/EnclcyopediaCoptica</u> (accessed October, 2006)

Encyclopedia of Islam, vol. VII, Leiden, E.J. Brill, 1993.

Kabbani, Sheik Hisham and Laleh Bakhtiar, *Encyclopedia of Muhammad's Women Companions*, Chicago, Kazi Pub., 1998.

Oxford Dictionary of Byzantium, Oxford University Press, 1991.

Wehr, Hans, *A Dictionary of Modern Written Arabic*, ed., J. Milton Cowan. London, MacDonald & Evans Ltd., 1974.

Poetry

Boethius, "Book II, Poem VII: Love is Lord of All" *The Consolation of Philosophy*, http://www9.georgetown.edu/faculty/jod/boethius/jkok/list_t.htm, (accessed Jan, 2007).

Boland, Eavan, "Domestic Interior," *Outside History*, New York, W.W. Norton, 1990.

Clifton, Lucille, "Far Memory, 7 Gloria Mundi," *The Book of Light*, Port Townsend, WA, Copper Canyon Press, 1993.

Darwish, Mamoud, "Here the Birds' Journey Ends," trans. by Fady Joudah, The New Yorker, August 25, 2008

Gilbert, Jack, "A Brief for the Defense," *Refusing Heaven*, New York, Alfred Knopf, 2005.

McHugh, Heather, "Wise Ease," *The Father of the Predicaments*, Middletown, Wesleyan University Press, 1999.

Nye, Naomi Shihab, "Kindness," *Words Under the Words: Selected Poems*, Portland, The Eighth Mountain Press, 1995.

Ostriker, Alicia, "Return of the Mothers," *The Nakedness of the Fathers: Biblical Visions and Revisions*, New Brunswick, N.J. Rudgers University Press, 1994.

Rumi, Mevlana Jalaluddin, *Open Secret, Versions of Rumi*, trans., John Moyne and Coleman Barks, Putney Vermont, Threshold Books, 1984.

Stafford, Kim, *Early Morning, Remembering My Father, William Stafford*, St Paul, Greywolf Press, 2002.

Endnotes

In this book, all citations from the Qur'an will be taken from *The Message of the Qur'an*, trans. by Muhammad Asad, Bristol, The Book Foundation, 2003, unless specified.

1   "The new Rule," *Open Secret, Versions of Rumi,* trans. John Moyne and Coleman Barks, p.45.

2   Hazrat Inayat Khan, *The Heart of Sufism*, (unpublished essay) p. 4 and *The Sufi Message of Hazrat Inayat Khan*, vol. IX, The Unity of Religious Ideals, p. 264.

3   The hadith in a strict sense, refer to the words and traditions of Prophet Muhammad. The hadith are also the body of traditions, explaining, for instance, how one washes before prayer, and other important guidelines not included in the Qur'an. In a larger sense the word "hadith" would include a narrative record of the sayings of Muhammad's Companions, including his wives. 'A'isha was known for repeating over 2,000 traditions. Eventually, the oral history was written down. These three respected historians — from the era of the eighth and nineth centuries — selected agreed upon hadith and compiled volumes, including nearly all of the mentioned hadith in this book. Their work is available in English translation: Muhammad Ibn Ishaq, Abu Ja'far Muhammad al-Tabari, and Muhammad Ibn Sa'd. There are other historical collections of the hadith, especially in the Shi'a tradition.

4   *Jahiliyya* is an important term, usually mistranslated as "the time of ignorance", instead, Ignaz Goldziher argues, he sees it as barbarism, not ignorance, citing *hilm* (gentleness), not *'ilm* (knowing) as the opposite term. He quotes an old Arab proverb: *The meek is the pack animal of the ferocious (al-halim matiyyat al-jahul.)* He devotes an entire chapter of his cited book to this subject: The Arabic root of *hilm* is *halama,* which means: to dream, muse or meditate on something. *Halim* means mild, gentle, and patient, and *halam* means the nipple (of the female breast). It can be said, then, that the doorway to "the milk of human kindness" is part of the remedy to the barbarian impulse!

5   Ibn Ishaq, *The Life of Muhammad*, trans: A. Guillaume, p. 59. This refers to Salama and woman's rights: The Prophet's great-grandfather Hashim,
from Mecca, married Salama, a woman from Medina. He returned home
and she remained behind to give birth and raise their child 'Abd al-Muttalib. When Hashim died, his brother went to bring the adolescent to live
with his father's family in Mecca. Salama and Hashim's brother negotiated
for three days. The boy said he would only leave his mother if she told him
to, which she finally did. So he was taken live in Mecca, and when he was
old, he raised his grandson, Muhammad.

6   The following sources refer to the harshness of 'Umar: See Kern, "The
Riddle of 'Umar al-Khattab, in Bukhari's Kitab al-Jami' as Sahih,"(Ph.D.
thesis, Harvard University, 1966) p.55 fn 109, p. 428 fn 61 (all these citations refer to hadith by Bukhari); Madelung, *The Succession to Muhammad*
p. 30 fn 7. Abbott, Nabia: *A'ishah, the Beloved of Mohammed*, (London,
Saqi Books, 1998) p.88 fn 19.

7   The young Khadija attended a festival where "something in the shape
of a man appeared…and then called out…Khadija ignored what he said but
did not treat him (harshly) as the other women did." Ibn Sa'd, *The Women
of Medina*, pp. 9-10. The same story is in al-Tabari, *The History of al-Tabari*,
vol. VI. "Muhammad at Mecca," p. 64. Al-'Uzza is one of the three primary goddesses worshipped in Mecca in the era before Islam. The others
are Manat and Allat. The name of her great-grandmother's mother, 'Atiqa b.
'Abdul 'Uzza, links this lineage with the shrine at Nakhlah, so it is probable
that her women ancestors paid tribute there.

8   Khadija has a record of six woman ancestors starting with her mother— Fatima b. Za'ida; her grandmother — Hala b. 'Abdu Manif; her great-
grandmother — al 'Arqa or Qibala b. Su'ayd; her great-great-grandmother
— 'Atiqa b. 'Abdul 'Uzza; her great-great-great-grandmother — al-Khuty or
Rayta b. Ka'b; her great-great-great-great-grandmother — Na'ila b. Hud-
hafa.The name of her niece, Umaya b. Ruqayya, is another indicator of
matriarchy. (*Bint* b. means "daughter of") Ibn Sa'd, p. 9.

9   Khadija's husbands were Abu Hala, and Atiq. It is said she had a son
named Hind and a daughter called Hinda.

10   'Abd al-Mutalib, Muhammad's grandfather, was the patriarch of the Hashim tribe, a wealthy man who re-discovered the Well of Zamzam. He was the "protector of Mecca," "lord of the camels" during the Abyssinian invasion, and father of ten sons. (Lings, *Muhammad*, p. 20). When Muhammad's father 'Abdullah died, Muhammad lost all opportunity of inheritance. His mother, Amina, came from a good family as well. She also died, and Muhammad was raised by his grandfather and then his uncle.

11   What age was Khadija really? Most likely she was younger than forty years old. Al-Tabari mentions in a footnote: "...according to some reports she was twenty-eight." vol. IX. p.127. Karen Armstrong writes, "She was probably somewhat younger (than 40 since she had 5 more children)." Armstrong, *Muhammad*, p.8.

12   There are some vestiges of controversy over the chance that the three oldest daughters of Khadija were children of a former husband and Muhammad only called them "his daughters" to be inclusive and explain his inordinate attention toward Fatima. This is the point of view of some Shi'a scholars.

13   Most sources conceal the fact that 'Uthman was married to another women (Ramla) at the same time he was married to the Prophet's daughters. Madelung, p. 364.

14   Nuha al-Abed, a woman I met in Damascus in 2003, told me the legend of the source of the conflict between the two tribes of Muhammad's family. Twins were born to Muhammad's great-great-grandfather, 'Abd al-Manaf. They say the boys were joined foot to forehead, and needed to be cut apart. As this was done, the doctor predicted that their blood would flow down through history. Hashim, Muhammad's ancestor, was the twin with the scarred foot, while 'Abd al-Shams bore the scar on his forehead. His son was Umayyah, the great-grandfather of 'Uthman.

15   The Prophet's daughter, Zaynab, speaks in the mosque (hadith): Ibn Sa'd, *The Women of Madina* p. 22; "I have given safe conduct to Abul-'As..." and in Lings, p.235.

16   History differs on dates and numbers of children. This version of Fatima's birth is based on a Syrian teaching story that assumes Khadija mar-

ried Muhammad at forty, and that Fatima was the last of seven children. It is likely that Khadija was younger than forty. The footnote 60 in al-Tabari *The History of al-Tabari,* vol. VI, "Muhammad at Mecca," p. 49 mentions seven children (the first two from her first marriage), with five by Muhammad, after age forty, (including a son who died at birth). However, Ibn Sa'd, *The Women of Madina,* p.13 relates that Fatima was born "while the Quraysh were re-building the Ka'ba. That was five years before prophethood." Al-Tabari concurs (*The History of al-Tabari,* vol. IX, "The Last Years of the Prophet" p. 128). This sets the time table back a decade, putting Fatima into a life of privilege for the first seven or so years of her life; then, as she grew toward adolescence her father plunged into his life's work, and her family life became increasingly austere and dangerous.

17   Uncle Waraqa predicted Muhammad's future. He said, "Oh, Khadija, there hath come unto him the greatest namus (meaning Gabriel) who came to Moses aforetime, and lo, he is the prophet of his people. Bid him be of good heart." Ibn Ishaq, *The Life of Muhammad, p. 107.* Uncle Waraqa studied prophetic science, was a mystic and a monotheist, some say, a Christian or *Hanif*— (one who searches for a pure monotheism). His words to Muhammad carried reassurance. Al-Tabari writes that Zayd b. 'Amr b. Nufayl spoke of prophet-predictions: "I expect a prophet from the descendants of Ishmael, in particular from the descendants of 'Abd al-Muttalib [Muhammad's grandfather]. I do not think that I shall live to see him, but I believe in him, proclaim the truth of his message, and testify that he is a prophet. If you live long enough to see him, give him my greetings. I shall inform you of his description, so that he will not be hidden from you. He is a man who is neither short nor tall, whose hair is neither abundant nor sparse, whose eyes are always red, and who has the seal of prophet-hood between his shoulders. His name is Ahmad, and this town is his birthplace and the place in which he will commence his mission. Then his people will drive him out and hate the message which he brings, and he will emigrate to Yathrib (Medina) and triumph." Al- Tabari, *The History of al-Tabari,* vol. VI, "Muhammad at Mecca," p. 64.

18   The tradition of the worship of stones in relation to monotheism is explained here. Peters, p. 12.

19   The first moments of the practice of *salat* are observed. Al-Tabari, The History of al-Tabari, vol. VI, "Muhammad at Mecca," p. 81.

20   The compelling power of the Qur'an in the Arabic language is illustrated here:

There's a story of the great Sufi master, Ibn 'Arabi, who as a child was in a coma, dying. A most beautiful being appeared to him. He asked, "Who are you?" The voice replied, "I am *Sura Ya Sin*" (verse 36), [the one his own father was saying at the foot of his bed]. The boy opened his eyes and was healed.

It is safe to say there are no miracles, as such, attributed to Muhammad. The Qur'an itself is the miracle of Islam. Another example of the power of those words is about 'Umar before he joined Muhammad. He was adamantly against Islam. One time he was scolding his sister, after he found her reciting verses from the Qur'an that she had memorized. She kept speaking the phrases. 'Umar stopped, listened, and on the spot wanted to take up the path he had sworn to eradicate, just on the strength of what he heard.

21   Recent destruction: Al-Tabari (ninth century historian) described the Prophet's house at that time. al-Tabari, *The History of al-Tabari*, Vol VI, "Muhammad at Mecca" p.50. In the current decade, disturbing news about Khadija's tomb and house being destroyed comes from this source: Dr. Sami Angawi, (Saudi Architect from an old Jeddah family descended from the Prophet) "Online News Hour with Jim Lehrer", 2/19/02, by correspondent Elizabeth Farnsworth from an interview: "The tomb of the first wife of the Prophet... was totally demolished and is gone because of certain viewpoints that this could lead to idolatry... (and) Again another site, which I worked on in discovering and actually digging, the house of the Prophet in Mecca." More recently, *Islamica Magazine*, Issue 15, 2006, ran an article and photos showing of Khadija's house and the destruction. It has been covered with sand and paved over. Only the photos remain. There are also photos of the bare Baqi' Cemetary in Medina, where most of the other wives were buried.

22   'Ali's words (hadith). Abbott, *A'isha the Beloved of Muhammed*, p. 33.

23   The Prophet's dream of 'A'isha (hadith). Lings, *Muhammad*, p. 106.

24 'A'isha and Angel Gabriel (hadith). Ibn Sa'd, *The Women of Madina*, p. 55.

25 'A'isha sees the Abyssinian woman dancing (hadith). Alim on CD-ROM, narrator al-Tirmidhi, 'A'isha hadith, #1565.

26 "For everything there is a polish that takes away rust, and the polish of the heart is *dhikr Allah*." (hadith). Lings, *Muhammad*, p. 328.

27 "... like matchfire in the back light." This is line from a poem written by Charles Wright, (the contemporary American poet) from the poem, "Bar Giamaica, 1959-1960 from his book *The Southern Cross*.

28 Asma' b. al-Numan was from an Eastern tribe (the Jawniyya). Her father wished an alliance with Muhammad, and so sealed the wedding agreement with his "beautiful daughter." 'A'isha and Hafsa tricked her, and she was sent back. Ibn Sa'd, *The Women of Madina*, p. 153.

29 Prophet Muhammad said — referring to 'A'isha and Hafsa: "They are the companions to the brothers of Yusuf [Joseph]. Their deviousness is immense."(hadith). Ibn Sa'd, Ibid., p. 103.

30 'A'isha snips at Muhammad (hadith). *Alim* on CD-ROM, Narrator al-Bukhari, 'A'isha hadith # 7.48.

31 From the story of Juwayriyya, 'A'isha describes her: "She was a most beautiful woman. She captivated every man who saw her...as soon as I saw her at the door of my room I took a dislike to her, for I knew he would see her as I saw her." (hadith). Ibn Ishaq, *The Life of Muhammad*, p. 493.

32 'A'isha is jealous of Khadija (hadith). Abbott, *A'isha, the Beloved of Mohammed* p. 48.

33 Muhammad enjoys being a parent while 'A'isha suffers from childlessness. (hadith). Lings, *Muhammad* p. 315.

34 Prophet Muhammad's last words were: *at-taruku li Allahi bi'adadi anfasi al-khala'iq*, Arabic reference is, *Traditions of the Prophet*, Jami' al-asrar, collection of non-canonical hadith. *Shi'a Rasa'il Ni'matullahi*; vol. 1, p. 177. Courtesy of Imam Bilal Hyde.

35   Regarding 'A'isha and her 2,210 hadith, how accurate are they? Abbott, *Aishah, the Beloved of Mohammed,* pp. 201, 202.

36   'A'isha's response to the chaos of 'Uthman's rule (hadith). Madelung, p. 101.

37   The full sentence of the *Sura* from the Qur'an [Q. 49:9] is: *If two parties among the Believers fall into a quarrel make ye peace between them: but if one of them transgresses beyond bounds against the other then fight ye (all) against the one who transgresses until it complies with the command of Allah; but if it complies then make peace between them with justice and be fair: for Allah loves those who are fair (and just).* Ibn al-Arabi (the Malaki scholar, not the Sufi master. It is not commonly known there were two men by this name.) *Ahkam Al-Quran,* vol.3, p.1536 (Abu Sulaiman).

38   The political climate after Caliph 'Uthman's death was complex: 'Ali and 'A'isha held opposing views. She blamed 'Ali for failing to go after the killers of 'Uthman, while he wished to move on, and offered amnesty for all. Aslan, *No god but God* p. 130. 'A'isha called for the removal of 'Ali as caliph 'Ali refused the title and instead took the name, "Commander of the Faithful," holding the position that the family (Ahl al-bayt) held the right to rule in Muhammad's place.

39   "Beware the barking dogs..." was, according to some accounts, something Muhammad had prophetically told 'A'isha years before (hadith). Abbott, *Aishah, the Beloved of Mohammed* p. 143.

40   This is a phrase that may have been yelled in battle as a great animal with a howdah fell heavily *al-hawdaj!* — the howdah, *al-Haddun!* — the heavy, tumbling, fall.

41   'A'isha's defeat in war closed doors on women in political learership. D.A. Spellberg, *Politics, Gender, and the Islamic Past,* p.106.

42   "I must help anyone not plan a war." This line by poet William Stafford from *Early Morning, Remembering My Father, William Stafford,* p.100.

43   'A'isha's consuming regret (hadith). Abbott, 173.

44   'A'isha weeps over Qur'anic verse (hadith): Ibn Sa'd, *The Women of Madina* p 56.

[Q. 33:33]. *And abide quietly in your homes and do not flaunt your charms as they used to flaunt them in the old days of pagan ignorance; and be constant in prayer (salat), and render the purifying dues (zakat), and pay heed unto God and his Apostle; for God only wants to remove from you all that might be loathsome, O you members of the Prophet's household, and to purify you to utmost purity.*

45   'A'isha's last words (hadith). Ibn Sa'd, *The Women of Madina* p. 52.

46   Muhammad's well-known moment with Zaynab (hadith). Al-Tabari, *The History of al-Tabari*, vol.. XXXIX, "Biographies of the Prophet's Companions and their Successors," p.181.

47   Fariduddin 'Attar, 12th c. Persian mystic, is the man who wrote *The Conference of the Birds*. The hoopoe leads the other birds as an allegory of the teacher leading his students to self-knowledge. 'Attar is also mentioned in Reza Aslan, *No god but God,* p. 206.

48   There are two responses to what took place between Muhammad and Zaynab. One takes the view that Muhammad married her for political reasons because Zaynab, Muhammad's cousin, had family connections to the Meccan leader and enemy, Abu Sufyan. Watt, *Muhammad at Medina* p. 330. The second sees attraction followed by marriage. Al-Tabari, *The History of al-Tabari*, vol.VIII, "The Victory of Islam, Muhammad at Medina," p. 2.

49   Anas tells "the most extraordinary thing he saw..."(hadith). Ibn Sa'd, *The Women of Madina.* vol. VIII, p 75.

50   Lings, *A Sufi Saint in the Twentieth Century*, p. 211. These are the words of Shaykh Ahmad Al-'Alawi.

51   Umm Salama speaks of Zaynab. (hadith). ibid., p. 74.

52   'A'isha's most well known statement on Zaynab (hadith). *The Alim on CD-ROM.* Narrator, Sahih Muslim. 'A'isha hadith #1122.

53   Some say these "People of the Bench" or the "intimate friends of Allah" are early Sufis. They are also itinerants who arrived to be in the larger group around Muhammad, and were supported with donations of meals and clothing. In return, they chanted constantly the names of Allah. The Arabic, *muqarabun,* means, "one who comes close or near"(to Allah), the root is *qaraba.*

54   Zaynab speaks of her family connection (hadith). Al-Tabari, *The History of al-Tabari*, vol. XXXIX, "Biographies of the Prophet's Companions and their Successors," p. 182.

55   Al-Tabari, *The History of al-Tabari*, vol. IX "The Last Years of the Prophet"p.134. In this phrase, *(akramu kunna waliyyan wa akramu kunna safi ran)* Zaynab boasts that God is her nearest friend *(waliyy),* who gave her away in marriage and that Angel Gabriel is the intermediary.

56   Zaynab as the first wife to follow Muhammad in death (hadith): Ibn Sa'd *The Women of Madina* p. 77.

57   *Husband, your breath smells of manna gum.* and *I have drunk honey with Zaynab b. Jahsh. I won't do it again.* (Hadith from the Alim, Narrator, Bukhari. 6.434). *Why do you make forbidden what Allah has made lawful for you?* [Q. 66:1–5]. "Messenger of Allah, may this sweeten our days and nights." *(poetic line by the author.)*

58   Zaynab's death request (hadith). Ibn Sa'd, *The Women of Madina* p. 78.

59   "Hind," is another name for Umm Salama. Her grandfather was Walid al-Mughira, chief of the prominent Makhzum clan, the patriarch of Mecca who became instantly famous as the only man fearless enough to take a pickaxe to the old Ka'ba, when the rebuilding happened. It may be noteworthy from the matriarchal perspective that Martin Lings in his biography of Muhammad does not mention Hind's *father* by name, only her mother, 'Atiqa b. 'Amir b. Rabia of Kinana. Hind's husband 'Abdullah b. 'Abd al-Asad (Abu Salama) was the son of Muhammad's aunt Barra b. 'Abd al-Muttalib.

60   Abyssinia was an empire including present day Ethiopia, Eritheia, Nubia and Sudan. It was the legendary resting place of the Ark of the Covenant and the palace and pools of the Queen of Sheba. For the last centuries before Muhammad, the country was a trading partner with the Byzantine Empire as well as the East. Al-Tabari mentions (in *The History of al-Tabari*, Vol VI, "Muhammad at Mecca", p. 16) the business treaties forged — at the time of Hashim — with Syria, Persia and Yemen as well as Abyssinia. The good will from that era emboldened Muhammad to request refuge there for his family and followers.

61   The Negus gave his battle spear to al-Zubayr, one of the Arab immigrants who witnessed the battle the Abyssinian King fought on the west side of the Nile. Al-Zubayr gave it to Muhammad, who presented it to Bilal, his Abyssinian Meccan *muezzin* (the one who leads the call to prayer). It was used five times a day to indicate the direction of prayer. When the Negus died in 630, we are told the Prophet grieved for him.

62   Ramla (Umm Habiba) was from the influencial clan, Banu 'Abd al-Shams. Her father was Abu Sufyan, Muhammad's most powerful opponent. Her husband, 'Ubaydullah was a cousin of the Prophet, brother of Zaynab b. Jahsh, Muhammad's wife.

63   How Hind became Umm Salama: *Kunya* means honorific title. In Arab culture the child was so valued that the mother — Hind — became Umm (mother of) her son Salama, and his father too became known as Abu (father of) Salama. Ramla became Umm Habiba, named for her daughter, Habiba.

64   The exiles traveled to the Red Sea and went by boat to Adulis now on the coast of Eritrea. Munro-Hay, *Aksum, An African Civilization of Late Antiquity*, describes the journey as passing through 3 climatic zones through what was then dense forests and wild rock formations into present day Ethiopia.

65   The exiles comment on the hospitality they received (hadith). Ibn Ishaq, *The Life of Muhammad*, p. 150.

66   According to history, there was a painting of Mary and Jesus in the Ka'ba. Martin Lings, *Muhammad*, p. 300. This most likely remained until 683, when the building was partially demolished.

67   Ja'far defends Muhammad, and recites verses from the Sura of Mary [Q. 19:16–21](hadith). Lings, Ibid., p.83.

68   The Negus responds to Ja'far (hadith). Lings, Ibid., p.84.

69   Stuart Munroe-Hay discusses the flora and fauna: "Aksum ... offers extreme contrasts of winter and summer... Vegetation and streams abound, and there must have been a considerable variety of wildlife in ancient times. Alvares, who described part of his journey as passing 'through mountains and devilish jungle', populated his jungle with lions, elephants, tigers, leopards..." Aksum, *An African Civilization of Late Antiquity*, Chapter 3, p. 26.

70   Kern gives a brilliant translation from the hadith describing Umm Salama responding to 'Umar's rough behavior toward the wives. Linda Lee Kern, *The Riddle of 'Umar al-Kitab*, pp. 295, 296.

71   [Q. 22:39–40]. *Permission to fight is given to those who fight because they have been wronged; and God is able to give them victory. Those who have been driven from their homes unjustly, for no cause other than their saying: Our lord is God.* The word *jihad* "striving," has an inner and outer form. As "lesser *jihad*" it refers directly to the defense strategies of Muhammad's *umma,* and protection from defeat. War was for them at that time, largely defensive. The "greater *jihad*" refers to the self-reflective inner war against the *nafs,* (ego).

72   More than one thousand Companions made the *Ridwan* Pledge: an oath of allegiance, a strong agreement with Muhammad. They swore to honor him, and his actions; then nearly every one of the men was tested with doubt when Muhammad asked them to accept the peace treaty he created. They would not do what he told them. He asked Umm Salama how to proceed. Lings, *Muhammad*, pp. 252-256.

73   A victory! The first great peace treaty in Arab history. Ibn Ishaq, *The Life of Muhammad* p. 507.

74   These are the words the Prophet spoke as he broke the idols; also in the Qur'an: [Q. 17: 81]. For the entire story of breaking the idols, see Martin Lings, *Muhammad*, pp. 297-303.

75   It is said that Ibn Hajar al-Asqalani, the fifteenth century hadith scholar in his *Tahdhib al-Tahdhib*, has given the names of at least thirty-two great scholars who learned hadith from Umm Salama, and then narrated them on her authority. Marwan and many like him turned to her to learn various issues and jurisprudence. Fida Hussain Malik says says she handed down 378 hadith. Malik, *Wives of the Holy Prophet*, p. 139.

76   The calamity in this passage refers to Surah 101 in the Qur'an: al-Qari'a. Karbala is the place Husayn, grandson of the Prophet, was martyred. His tomb in Iraq is revered by Muslims today. Umm Salama's dream; I've come to believe that this is a story from the Shia tradition of hadith, which is why it is difficult to duplicate in my mostly Sunni-based research. Malik, *Ibid.*, p.123.

77   [Q. 101:3–4].

78   This quote is from *The Bible*, 21:9,10,14. *The Wilderness of Beersheba*. The story is that Sarah had Hagar and her son Ishmael cast out into the desert. Sarah is later seen as Jewish, while Hagar is the Mother of Muslims, wronged by the wife of a Hebrew Prophet.

79   Hagar's words come from hadith. Alim on CD-ROM, Narrator al-Bukhari, Ibn 'Abbas Hadith #4.584.

80   Sarah, Hagar and Abraham, are the famous ancestors of the People of the Book (Jews, Christians and Muslims). In the Bible, Sarah is not glossed over, but shown as a jealous, competitive woman in this verse from Genesis. Other stories say that Ishmael was unruly and it was due to his behavior that they were expelled. The Qur'an tells of the angels disguised as strangers coming to Abraham and Sarah. They were offered food, but declined and the angels told Abraham "his wife" would give birth to "a wise son." [Q. 51:23–29]. This is the moment of the famous laugh, in Judaic history, as in "Sarah laughed" at the idea that at age 89, she could have a child. Hagar is mentioned as "a slave girl," the compensation gift from an Egyptian "pagan ruler" [Pharaoh] for making sexual advances to Sarah, when Abraham and

Sarah were his guests. (The *Alim*, the story of Ibrahim; also Bukhari, Abu Huraira, 3:803).

One Jewish *midrash* explains that Hagar was daughter of Pharaoh and that she was impressed with Abraham's knowledge and power and asked to go as Sarah's maid, but later was disdainful of Sarah, hence the expulsion. (The Qur'an fails to name either Sarah or Hagar by name). A matriarcal *midrash* gives Hagar the assignment from God to "found a nation." To do this she gets the help of Sarah, who pretends to get her expelled so she can fulfill her destiny. (Told by Rabbi Phyllis Berman at the Seven Pillars Inauguration. New Lebanon, N.Y., September, 2008)

81   A spring appeared where Ishmael's heel struck the earth, and miraculously saved them. It became the well of Zamzam in Mecca, re-discovered after centuries by Muhammad's grandfather, 'Abd al-Muttalib. *[A]nd I will make him [Ishmael] a great nation.* (Genesis, 17:20). Regarding the Arabic legends of Abraham and the Ka'ba, Martin Lings writes (*Muhammad*, p. 42): "The rite of prostrating oneself to God in the direction of the Holy House had been performed there since the time of Abraham and Ishmael. *And when Abraham and Ishmael were raising the foundations of the Temple (Ka'ba), [they prayed:] 'Oh our Sustainer! Out of our offspring a community that shall surrender itself unto Thee. Raise up from the midst of our offspring an apostle from among themselves, who shall convey unto them thy messages, and impart unto them revelation as well as wisdom...* [Q. 2:127–129].

82   Mention of the anti-Jewish sentiments of Muhammad's biographers: Reza Aslan, *No god but God*, pp. 98-100. The following Qur'anic verses support brotherhood of people of the Book: *We believe in God and in that which has been bestowed from on high upon us, and that which has been bestowed upon Abraham and Ishmael and Isaac and Jacob and their descendants, and that which has been vouchsafed by their Sustainer unto Moses and Jesus and all the [other] prophets; we make no distinction between any of them.* [Q. 3:84]; and this from the early days of Medina: *Verily, those who have attained to faith [in this divine writ] as well as those who follow the Jewish faith, and the Christians, and the Sabians — all who believe in God and the Last Day and do righteous deeds — shall have their reward with their Sustainer; and no fear need they have, and neither shall they grieve.* [Q. 2:62].

83   Regarding Rayhana — "The Prophet took her and set her free and married her"(hadith). Al-Tabari, vol.XXXIX, "Biographies of the Prophet's Companions and their Successors," p.165; Also Ibn Sa'd, *The Women of Madina,* p. 153. According to another version, she refused to marry him and preferred to be his concubine. (al-Tabari footnote 742), [same page].

84   Within Judiasm the *Bet Midrash* (House of Study) was the main place for the study of the Law and all interests that surrounded its investigation. The sanctity of the *bet midrash* was considered greater than that of the synagogue (*bet knesset*), and rabbis often preferred to pray in the *Bet Midrash* rather than the synagogue.) Ibn Ishaq, *The Life of Muhammad,* p. 255: This midrash story has come down in the many discussions between the rabbis and Muhammad; the rabbis ask him to answer four questions (riddles), and if he does so correctly they will follow him. The first question is about the why a boy resembles his mother when the semen comes from the man. The second: tell us about your sleep. The third: tell us about what Israel voluntarily forbade himself. The fourth: tell us about spirit. Muhammad answers the first three correctly, then mentioned Angel Gabriel as the embodiment of the Spirit of God. The rabbis reply, "O Muhammad, he (Gabriel) is an enemy to us, and angel who comes only with violence and the shedding of blood, and were it not for that, we would follow you". (This may have been added to make the Jews look bad.)

There were several Muslims in the *umma* who had extensive knowledge of the Torah, such as Ibn 'Abbas, 'Ali, and Salman al-Farisi. Muhammad's scribe, Zayd b. Thabit "learned *al-Yahudiyya* in a Bet Midrash...in order to read Jewish material." Newby, p. 66. On the other hand, there's a nasty story of how Abu Bakr went to a Bet Midrash and became enraged, striking the rabbi hard in the face because he committed "blasphemy"(hadith). Ibn Ishaq p. 263. This could not have sat well with the Jewish community.

One belief system that created antagonism and gave Judaism a bad reputation among the new Muslims was an apocalyptic add-on practiced in Arabia at the time. For example the *Rabbinites,* as this sect was called, had embraced a "creator angel" called by some "Metatron". He was a transformation of biblical Enoch, called "Prince of the Countenance" because he had looked on the face of God. He had returned to earth as a messenger-angel. Muhammad condemned this belief as not monotheism, but rather *shirk* (ascribing partners to God). Newby p.60

85   So-called "friends" of Muhammad were a serious problem. *munafiq-in*: Ar. root: *nafaqa* translates as "to sell well, be a successful merchant" also, "to undermine or tunnel", as in the hole of a rat or mouse, also it carries the meaning — to be "two faced". Muhammad made use of the multiple meanings. The Qur'an speaks of them: *God will mark out those who have attained to faith, and certainly, will mark out the munafiqum.* [Q. 29:11], and, *God imposes suffering on the hypocrites, both men and women as well as on the men and women who ascribe divinity to aught beside Him.* [Q. 33:73]. This one is powerful: *On that day (the hereafter), shall the munafiqum, both men and women speak unto those who have attained to faith: 'Wait for us! Let us have a ray of light from your light!' But they will be told, 'turn back and seek a light of your own!'* [Q. 57:13].

86   This Constitution proposed the costs of defending Medina be divided equally among all city residents and further, guaranteed religious freedom to Jews and pagans as well as Muslims. Most of the clan leaders signed it. As consequence of betrayal, the Bana Qaynuqa and the Bana Nadir were expelled from Medina and their property, confiscated.

87   The description of dividing the prisoners after the Battle of the Trench is in this hadith: Lings p. 231.

88   Rayhana is not generally on the list of Muhammad's wives. However, according to the sources that follow here, she was married to the Prophet. Muhammad married her and had a screen set up for her while in the presence of the men, showing that he had not just taken her as concubine. Since she was the wife and daughter of once powerful enemies, he wanted his soldiers to see he had honored her. Ibn Sa'd, p. 92, 94. Her discription of the place and year of marriage is noted: Ibn Kathir, *The Life of the Prophet Muhammad*, vol. IV, pp. 434, 435. More information on Rayhana can be found here: Al-Tabari, vol.XXXIX, "Biographies of the Prophet's Companions and their Successors," p.165.

89   Rayhana is described as beautiful, and sad about her previous husband (hadith). Ibn Sa'd, p. 92. The statement of her marriage is from the hadith of Az-Zuhri.

90   Safiyya b. Huyayy b. Akhtab was from the Khazraj and Bana Nadir on her father's side and her mother belonged to the Bana Qurayzah and

was the sister of Rifa'ah Bana Samaw'al, one of the two men who converted to Islam from the clan of Qurayzah. Safiyya was married three times, the second time to Kinanah b. ar-Rabi an-Nadiri, the third to Muhammad.

91   Safiyya's wedding night (hadith). Ibn Sa'd, p. 89 (Abu Hurayra). Also, al-Tabari, vol. 39, p.185.

92   This "falling story" (hadith) is in *Alim* on CD-ROM, Narrator al-Bukhari, Anas b. Malik hadith # 8:204.

93   'A'isha's hadith on Zaynab's refusal (hadith). Ibn Sa'd p. 90.

94   Muhammad defends Safiyya in front of the other wives (hadith). Ibid., p. 91.

95   This is regarding alliances: Sa'id b. al-Musayyab tells that Safiyya gave some gold earrings to Fatima and some women with her(hadith). Ibid., p. 90.

96   Muhammad feels "near to the son of Mary" (hadith). *Alim* on *CD-ROM,* Narrator al-Bukhari, Abu Huraira hadith #4.652.

97   Christian monk predicts (hadith). Abu Ja'far Muhammad al-Tabari, *The History of al-Tabari*, vol.VI, "Muhammad at Mecca," p.45. The monk's name was Bahira.

98   Fresco of Mary and Jesus in the Ka'ba is an important link between Christians and Muslims. Reza Aslan, *No god but God*, p. 106, "The various depictions of gods and prophets, such as that of Abraham holding diving-ing rods, were all washed away with Zamzam water; all, that is except for the one of Jesus and his mother, Mary. This image the Prophet put his hand over, with reverence, saying, "Wash out all except what is beneath my hands." This tradition of sparing the images of Mary and Jesus is found in Martin Lings, *Muhammad*, p. 300. Ibn Ishaq's *Life of Muhammad* posits in a footnote that this (description) was amended to say "all the pictures were obliterated" as a later tradition. p. 552. (also, see Poem: *Mariya's vision,* which poetically links Marya with this story, but has no historical basis).

99   Christian leaders corresponded with Muhammad. The word from the Najran Bishop may have been in response to the letter from Muhammad:

*...the Bishop of b. al-Harith b. Ka'b and the bishops of Najran and the priests
and those who followed them and their monks, that for all their churches, ser-
vices and monastic practices, few or many, they have the protection (jiwar) of
God and His Messenger* (hadith). Ibn Ishaq, p. 271.

In another letter the strong connection between Muhammad and the
Christians is mentioned. From Muhammad's letter to Dughatir the Bishop,
*Peace to him who believes. Furthermore, Jesus son of Mary is the spirit of God
and His word; he placed it in Mary the pure. I believe in God and what was
revealed to us and what was revealed to Abraham, Ishmael, Isaac and Jacob,
and to the Israelites (asbat), and what was given to Moses and Jesus, and what
was given to the prophets from their Lord. We do not distinguish between any of
them (count some superior to others). We are surrendered (muslimun) to Him.
Peace be upon him who follows the guidance.* He sent this by Dihyah b. Khali-
fah al-Kalbi. Watt, p. 318 (from Ibn Sa'd.)

100 The *Negus* responded to the letter sent by Muhammad saying that
what the Qur'an says about Jesus and Mary is what he believes, and that he
accepts Muhammad and is sending him his son (and 60 Ethiopians who
perished in the Red Sea on the journey). al-Tabari, *The History of al-Tabari*,
vol. VIII, "The Victory of Islam," p. 108.

101 Hadith mentioning Jesus in a positive way. *Alim on CD-ROM*, Narrator al-Bukhari, Ubada hadith # 4.644.

102 The editors of this 1993 edition of *The Encyclopedia of Islam* are so
frustrated with the lack of solid information between The Persian occupation of Egypt and the arrival of the Muslim army — all in less than a decade
— that they suggest that the two sisters, Mariya and Shirin, may not have
existed in Egypt or at all. This entry (Mariya the Copt) mentions instead
they may have been from the royal family of Persia!

Even the identity of the "Patriarch of Alexandria" who received the
Prophet's letter in 628, is uncertain. Regarding Benjamin the thirty-eighth
Patriarch: He brought a sense of unity among Coptic churches, but was
in hiding in Upper Egypt between 626 and 631. (Mena of Nikiou, p.15).
Regarding Cyrus: The Encyclopedia of Islam, vol. VII says, "Cyrus arrived
in Egypt in 631... if correct, this account places the mission in 627-628 (of
Mariya's meeting with the Prophet, so Cyrus was not the Muqawqis."

103   Mariya al-Qibtiyya is not commonly said to have married the Prophet, but certainly everyone gave her the same title of respect as the Prophet's wives, *Umm al-Muminin* (Mother of the Believers). She ended up in the court of the Muqawqis as a young girl. She arrived in Medina to join the Prophet's household just after the Prophet returned from the treaty with Quraysh which was contracted at al-Hudaybiya. Ibn Kathir, in his biography of the Prophet, names her home as the Upper Egypt town (*kurat*) called Anda'. Ibn Kathir, *The Life of the Prophet Muhammad*, vol. I, p. 191.

104   The list of what the Muqawqis sent to Muhammad (hadith). al-Tabari vol., XXXIX p.193.

105   Coptic names of the months — Thout to Kioahk (flood season), Tobe to Paremonde (planting season), Pachons to Mesore (harvest).

106   Hasan b. Thabit was a poet in the *umma*. Poets of that time were vital communicators who could deliver support or scandal. Hasan had participated in spreading rumors of 'A'isha during her accusations and he was disciplined for his misinformation. Martin Lings writes, p. 246, "After a certain time had elapsed, (he, Muhammad) showed great generosity to Hasan." It is clear from this that 'A'isha may not have cared for Hasan — or his concubine, Shirin.

107   Mariya's status: 1. The screen (hadith). Ibn Sa'd, p. 149. 2. There are hadith references to a "marriage" between Mariya and Muhammad, but they are not reliable sources. This one I was unable to verify, but I'm noting it because it may be useful. Al-Hakim al-Naysapouri, Al-Mustadrak 'ala al-Sahihayn, Ed., Dr. Yusuf Mar'ashli, vol. IV. Lebanon, Dar al-Ma'rifa Pub., p. 86.

108   Why the wives were jealous of Mariya (hadith). Ibn Sa'd, p. 149.

109   Hafsa's words about Mariya (hadith). Ibn Sa'd, p. 149.

110   The fresco of Mary and Jesus in the Ka'ba is refered to in Lings, p. 300. This narrative poem puts Mariya and her garden together with the incident in the Ka'ba during the time of the breaking of the idols, and draws on the deep connection of Christian women especially, to Mary. In actuality, there is no extant hadith linking Mariya to the Mother of Jesus.

111   "Her son has freed her…" (hadith). Ibn Saʻd p. 150, 151.

112   Muhammad's words, "Take care of the Copts…"(hadith). Ibid., p. 150.

113   The History of the Coptic Orthodox Church (on-line) states connection to Muhammad. http://st-takla.org/Coptic-church-1.html

114   Reza Aslan, p.3, describes al ʻUzza as the powerful goddess known as Isis and Aphrodite by Egypt and Greece, respectively.

115   "…the privacy of women" (hadith). Martin Lings, *Muhammad*, p. 117.

116   ʻAʼishaʼs words (hadith). *Alim on CD-ROM, narrator,* Sahih Muslim, ʻAʼisha, #703.

117   Regarding Sawda as a "heavy" woman (hadith). Ibn Saʻd, *The Women of Medina*, p. 41. Umar speaks of Sawda as "large"(hadith). Ibid., p. 24.

118   Sawdaʼs words to Muhammad (hadith). Ibn Saʻd, *The Women of Medina* p. 40.

119   Careful translation gives a deeper, more open meaning to the quote about women staying in their homes [Q. 33:33]. From Arthur Buehler: "qarna fi buyutikinn," meaning to abide quietly in your homes [then explaining how the vowel "a" can migrate to become an "i"], Tabari explains that the general reading of Kufa and Basra is "qirna fi buyutikinn" meaning "be among those who command respect and who have a God-inspired peace of mind — in your houses." Muhammad b. Jarir al-Tabari, *Jamiʼ al-bayan fi tafsir al-Qurʼan*, 30 vols. (Beirut: Dar al-Maʻrifa, 1980), vol. 22:3.

120   "There's no more news from heaven now" (hadith). *Alim on CD-ROM, narrator,* Sahih Muslim, hadith #1125.

121   Angel Gabrielʼs words to Muhammad about Hafsa (hadith).Ibn Saʻd pp. 58, 59.

122   Hafsa and Muhammad discuss intellectual topics (hadith). Fida Hussain Malik, *Wives of the Holy Prophet*, p. 131.

123　The Qur'an and Hafsa. In this lecture there is mention of Hafsa entrusted with the Qur'an. Muhammad Akram, "A Glimpse at Early Women Islamic Scholars."

124　Marwan sends for the Qur'an (hadith). *Alim on CD-ROM, narrator,* al-Bukhari, Anas b. Malik hadith #6:183-184.

125　Words describing Juwayyria (hadith). Al-Tabari, *The History of al-Tabari,* vol. XXXIX, "Biographies of the Prophet's Companions and their Successors," p. 183.

126　'A'isha's praises Juwayyria (hadith). Ibid. p. 183.

127　The Negus proposes marriage on behalf of Muhammad (hadith). Ibn Sa'd p. 68.

128　The Negus gifts Umm Habiba with scent. *Wars* may have been confused with *ward,* which means rose blossoms in Arabic. Civet is an animal product similar to musk. Ibid., p. 69.

129　The last years of the Abyssinian era. According to the historian Ibn Ishaq, there were two unsuccessful rebellions against the Negus in the eight years that the immigrants were in Ethiopia (153-155). When he died in 630, the year after Umm Habiba and the last immigrants left, it may have been in the town of Wegro, southeast of Aksum. His position had weakened greatly with the Persian occupation of Egypt and the earlier defeat in Yemen of King Kaleb. Red Sea trade, and with it prosperity ceased. It is guessed that more Abyssinian internal revolts followed. Aksum, after centuries of great power, was abandoned and the era of the empire was over. "Because no Muslim historians that I've discovered discuss the fall of the Capitol City of the Empire, it is likely that the exiles made it out just before its collapse." (Munro-Hay, p. 620.)

130　Abu Sufyan replied with a proverb, "That stallion's nose is not to be restrained." This was camel breeding talk. The camel with an inferior pedigree would be struck on the nose by the breeder, signifying rejection. This "camel"(Muhammad) passed the test. Al-Tabari, *The History of al-Tabari,* vol. VIII, *The Victory of Islam* p. 110, note 467.

131 Abu Sufyan comes to Umm Habiba's room (hadith). Lings, *Muhammad*, p. 291.

132 The story of Abu Safyan barging into his daughter's room is hadith from Ibn Ishaq, p.543. [Q. 112:1] *Qul Huwal-lahu Ahad*, "Say, Only Allah."

133 Hafsa talks back to Muhammad (hadith). Linda Lee Kern, *The Riddle of 'Umar b. al-Khattab*, p.292.

134 Asma's beauty (hadith), Ibn Sa'd, p. 103. Al-Tabari, *The History of al-Tabari,* vol. XXXIX, "Biographies of the Prophet's Companions and their Successors," p. 191.

135 Asma's life: other sources say that since she was never really a wife, she did remarry. Asma''s home, *ash-Sharba* in the Najd was the region East of Medina. Ibn Sa'd. p. 104; According to Ibn 'Abbas, she was never called Mother of the Faithful, never had a partition set up, so she did marry much later, a man named al-Muhajir b. Abi Umayya. 'Umar disapproved of this. Also, there is a poem in the 'A'isha chapter called "My Wives are like the Brothers of Joseph," telling this same story

136 The last line, "the fall is lifelong, to the knees" is by poet Heather McHugh.

137 Here the names of dates and *nuquul (naql)* sweets, desert fruits. *Ba* and *Raw* are Arabic consonants from Maymuna's given name, Barra b. al Harith. *Deglet Noor* "pieces of light," is a popular kind of date. *Sukkari* means sugar. Brands from Western Arabian date farms are *Anbara* "perfumed with ambergris" and *Safwi* "the best".

138 Earlier in the poem is a reference to 'A'isha as a young girl. Chapter 3 ('A'isha), endnote 25. Here is 'A'isha, watching the dancers in the Mosque, illustrating how relaxed Muhammad was with spontaneous expression. Later on, rules would make this a punishable offense, to dance in a mosque. The other stories are about his wives, Umm Salama (at Hudaybiah) and Zaynab b. Jahsh.

139   The Qur'an never singles woman out as the initiator or temptress. Satan was the catalyst, for both Eve and Adam. Their fall was equal. The expulsion "opens up the possibility for all humanity to receive immeasurably of God's Mercy and to acquire permanent salvation..." Barlas, p. 139. Many Muslim ideas about women are misogyny, not words of the Qur'an.

140   Buldozers have turned the Cemetary of the Wives to dirt and pebbles, while cement covers many grave sites. *Islamica Magazine* has photos of the Baqi' Cemetary and Khadija's grave (endnote 21).

141   "... under the feet of the mothers" is considered the words of Prophet Muhammad and attributed to the hadith collection of an-Nasai.

142   *din* —An important note here: *Din* is usually translated "faith" or "religion," but means in a mystical sense, the "path of return to Allah."